21ST CENTURY FILM STUDENT

. . . .

PRIMER
EVERYTHING YOU NEED TO KNOW AND DO BEFORE YOU GO TO FILM SCHOOL

JOHN POZER

21st Century Film Student PRIMER
Copyright © 2018 by John Pozer

Cover Design: Matthew Gagnon
www.matthewgagnon.ca
Editors: Justin Gagnon & Matthew Gagnon
Executive Editor: Oscar Pietri

Available at special discounts when purchased
in bulk for educational use. For inquiries, please
visit www.pozervision.com, or send an email
to 21stcenturyfilmstudent@gmail.com

Tellwell Talent
www.tellwell.ca

ISBN
978-0-2288-0231-0 (Paperback)
978-0-2288-0232-7 (eBook)

PRIMER

READER REVIEWS

"John Pozer's book PRIMER is critical reading for anyone considering attending a film school. As a film teacher in a public high school, I have seen too many students commit to a very expensive education without fully preparing to make the most of it. PRIMER breaks down every possible aspect of attending film school and provides valuable insights in how to squeeze the most out of an intensive and competitive educational process. This book is the best money any future film student (or parent of a film student!) could possibly spend. Rarely do post-secondary students enter their programs fully prepared to get their full money's worth. This rare book allows film students — any student really — to do just that. There are numerous suggestions and exercises specifically designed to ensure the student understands what they can do to be ready to go on Day 1 of their film school career. I can only beg parents and future film students to get this book as early as possible — grade 10 even — and dig in right away — it will make a huge difference. HIGHLY RECOMMENDED!"

- Robert French, Film Teacher, Brookswood
Secondary School/Producer: The Hamster Cage,
See Grace Fly; Screenwriter: Noroc

"If you are a prospective film student, or the parent of one, you both want to read this book. I wish I had."

- Oscar Pietri, Vancouver Film School, Film
Production Alumni 2012, Producer/Executive Editor

"This is the book every aspiring film student should read, a true eye-opener about what to expect when going to film school and the nature of the industry they're hoping to become a part of. Also a great read for recent graduates or filmmakers already on their path to professional success, this book will help you re-evaluate what you've learned and motivate you to create."

- Olga Maldonado, Voice Actor.

"A must-read for both students of film and amateur filmmakers. The insightful tips and practical examples given will help filmmakers make informed decisions in both their careers and artistic endeavors."

- Christopher Cowden, Filmmaker & Educator

"John Pozer taught me much of what I know about film, and reading PRIMER is like taking his class all over again. It's simple, insightful, and to-the-point. It offers good advice without being needlessly prescriptive. Best of all, it gives you the chance to reflect before you take the plunge. Nobody can tell you if film school is right for you, but Pozer's insight can guide you to the right place to make that call."

- Tony Zhou, Co-Writer/Director/Editor:
Every Frame a Painting

In loving memory of my parents, Doris & Bill Pozer.

And to my lovely wife, Lorraine. Thank

you for sowing seeds of wonder.

TABLE OF CONTENTS

There are three things that matter

in film school: ideas, ideas, ideas.

JOHN POZER

INTRODUCTION

One hundred years ago, people were lining up to enroll in the first-ever film school. The teachers were pioneering filmmakers and avant-garde theorists whose ideas influenced cinema enthusiasts around the world. The original prototype for formal film education was founded at the state-run Moscow Film School. The model quickly spread to neighbouring countries and training the new generation of filmmakers became a priority for the development of national identities.

One hundred years later, through many changes and challenges, film education has flourished. World-class programs are a magnet for creativity, attracting some of the most renowned artists of modern times. But film schools are more than gathering places for collaborative talents: they are vital to the advancement of the art form, cinematic movements and cultural revolutions.

Cinema has captivated the world's imagination for over a century. It has secured a global audience across many generations, and opportunities in the motion picture industry have never been greater. Film schools, however, have seen the cost of education and the competition for enrolment result in larger classes, shorter programs, and fewer full-time instructors. While these changes benefit the bottom line of school budgets, they also threaten to erode the transfer of knowledge and the serious study of cinema.

The 21st century film student should not be deterred. All of the information and everything you need to know in order to make a great movie is readily available. There has never been a more dynamic time to be in film school.

If you plan on pursuing a post-secondary film production education, I hope this book is the first step toward your best possible outcomes. If you're starting a program, or already in one, I hope to inspire you to make your best films. Whatever your situation, with this book in hand, I guarantee that you'll advance toward your cinematic ambitions more prepared, more confident, and more focused.

This book is a collection of ideas and strategies for re-thinking film education from the student perspective. It's about creativity, voice, storytelling, and how to get the most out of film school based on my years of experience as a filmmaker, film educator and film student. More importantly, this book is about you, your goals and your stories. The world is waiting for you to make your films. My hope is that you make them the best they can be.

John Pozer

2018

PART I

FIRST THOUGHTS

The film industry is demanding and competitive. You need to know what you're getting into—and you need to be ready for it.

I'm a believer in both instinct and preparation. I think you have to go in prepared and then you have to be able to throw away your preparation if something better occurs. But if you go in just with the vague hope that something brilliant will happen on the spot, you could be in a lot of trouble.

ROGER CORMAN

IS THIS BOOK FOR YOU?

This book is for readers of all ages who are curious to know more about film education; are enrolling in a film program; or have a loved one or friend who is.

This is the book I wish I had read before I went to film school.

The ideas here may have a broader appeal to readers interested in media, animation, game design or studio arts, but the content is geared toward those adventurous souls planning to explore the world of filmmaking through formal post-secondary education.

There are a few assumptions I'm going to make for anyone venturing further:

1. You are considering or already attending a film production program or want to know more about it;
2. You are interested in a degree, diploma or certificate as part of your career development;
3. You hope to establish relationships and career opportunities in film school;
4. You know that a career in film is challenging and competitive.

If you're looking ahead and wondering what you could learn or what training you could pursue that would lead to a job that is creative, rewarding and give you a sense of autonomy, then something in the film industry might be an appealing choice at first glance. However, careers in the film and television industries vary widely.

If you are already in the workforce, perhaps in a job or profession that hasn't brought happiness or satisfaction, filmmaking might seem like an exciting, social and lucrative alternative. Working your way up to a key position can take years. But for some, making a strong film—whether you're in film school or not—can be a game-changer, especially if it's invited to a major festival or wins awards.

If you're wondering if it's a good idea for you to enrol right now, this is a question we'll explore in the opening chapters. Given the time commitment and cost of some programs, pursuing an education in film could be one of the major decisions of your life.

The amount of time and money you should invest in your education deserves serious consideration. The three worst mistakes that anyone going to film school can make are borrowing too much money, signing up for the wrong program, and not being prepared.

Film is an art form. It continuously evolves and re-invents itself. It's a very competitive industry and there are no guarantees for success. Like most creative endeavours, no matter how thoroughly you plan or prepare there are always going to be dangers, risks and unexpected happenings on the road to realizing your goals.

I've had the pleasure of teaching students from all over the world, ranging from 17 to 61 years of age. Some were straight out of high school, others were adding skills to complement their ongoing careers. I've watched them make their films and tell their stories. I've seen tremendous accomplishments and crushing disappointments. One thing I know for certain: film school is not for the faint of heart.

Getting a degree or diploma can help with job placement and might create opportunities for career advancement, but to quote one of my favourite teachers, "No one is going to look at your diploma. Everyone wants to see your film."

HOW TO USE THIS BOOK

The purpose of this book is to provide you with information and ideas on how to create and navigate your best film school experience.

This is a *primer* for film school—not a *how-to* on film-making. There are many excellent books on how to write, direct and shoot films (and I recommend you read as many as you can!).

I believe in the transformative power of a first-class film education. Good gear, skilled educators and motivated classmates can create the synergy for a life-changing event. I've seen it happen—and I'd like it to happen more often.

Schools want successful students.

I've taught many talented filmmakers, but they didn't all graduate with their strongest creative work in hand. If your goal is to make films in a film production program, you need a plan. You need to design a roadmap with highlights of the major milestones you want to hit – and when you want to hit them. This book can help you do that.

Preparation can make or break a film. The same applies for film education. The preparation stage in filmmaking is called pre-production, or prep. It's vital for the successful management of a project. To apply this to your education, pre-production is everything that leads up to your first day of film school. Lead-time is critical: the more you have, the better—if you use it wisely.

If you know for certain that you are going to go to film school, next month or next year, you have an opportunity—starting now—to develop your plan, charge your creative batteries and make sure you are ready.

A thorough prep improves your chances for achieving your best outcomes. Every student I know (myself included) could have been better prepared to tell stories, work in teams and navigate the other challenges that happen in a filmmaking program. I know we would have made stronger films. And for me, that's the whole point.

The goal of a film production education is to produce work of merit. The biggest challenge for students is getting their best work realized—and finished—within the program timelines. Students need to have realistic plans and goals that make sense for the scope, scale and duration of their program.

Film school is like a runaway train: once you're in and it's moving, things get real—fast. You have to write, present, do the work and show it—on a deadline—while handling the pressures of other academic and personal responsibilities. To avoid being overwhelmed, and to get the best bang for your education buck, do the homework I'm handing out here before the bell rings for the first class.

The ideas and concepts in PRIMER will focus your intentions, tap into your creativity and empower your original voice—regardless of the type of films or specializations you're interested in. Doing the exercises will help you get ahead of the learning curve—and stay ahead. The films you study depend on your preferences and the ideas you generate are up to you.

Self-education and raising your baseline of film knowledge is totally possible: all it takes is discipline. If you work your way through this book and organize your creative assets, you'll be more than ready for every day of film school.

The life of a filmmaker is one of constant learning. If you're serious, your days ahead will be very busy.

THREE TRICKS FOR FILM SCHOOL

IT'S REAL TIME

The *first trick* is to set aside the time to study the classics before you go to film school. You'll be further ahead and stand a better chance to make good films if you know film history and the great filmmakers.

There are no benefits for shortcutting your knowledge of film. You build, develop and add to it with time and experience—frame-by-frame, scene-by-scene.

Cinema is a timepiece. It happens in real time, like music.

Everything you see and hear in a movie is a fixed stream of audiovisual information. You can't compress a 90-minute feature into a half hour. Nor can you study a classic by watching it out of the corner of your eye while checking your phone. It doesn't work that way: it never has.

You need to study films if you want to be a 21st century filmmaker. Studying a film means you have to experience the entire work to analyze what the filmmaking team is trying to do.

Studying the classics is not difficult, it just requires organization. You need to make a date with yourself where you find a time and place to watch without distractions or interruptions.

Skipping over film history creates unfortunate setbacks for new filmmakers who latch on to ideas only to find out, too late, that it's been done before—and done better. This is a lesson that you don't want to learn the hard way.

Study short films, too. This will be invaluable.

When it comes to making films in school, most programs are focused on the short form—under ten minutes—due mainly to costs and time constraints. Making long films demands a greater commitment: more footage, more editing, and more time.

When you're starting out and learning the craft, you want to make good short films, not mediocre long ones.

Making a film is an experience. So is watching one.

Start collecting experiences.

IT'S SPECIALIZED

The *second trick* is to figure out which specialization is the right career direction, and how you might realistically manage the transition from student to professional to achieve that goal.

Cinema is the synthesis of the arts, sciences and technology. At any point in time, there are countless actors, writers, artists, craftspeople and technicians vying for positions. There is a wide spectrum of careers in the film industry and the requisite skillsets don't necessarily overlap. Film education, like the industry, is built on specializations. This is one of the ways in which film programs differ from other arts programs.

It's not uncommon for students in the same class to focus on completely different aspects of filmmaking. This creates instructional challenges and curriculum design problems. For example, learning how to work with actors is one of the first steps for the student director, but a production designer doesn't require training for shaping an actor's performance.

Some schools offer programs that concentrate on specializations. Students apply for a stream of study, such as cinematography, directing, editing and so on. However, the majority of film schools cover it all: the technical knowledge and creative expertise that you need to make a movie from start to finish. Through this practical process of making films, students find their talents and eventually move into their areas of interest.

The connective tissue that holds all of these disparate departments and craftspeople together is the story of the film: storytelling resonates through every department in the production process. Not everyone who signs up for film school wants to be a writer, but scripts and stories are an essential component of filmmaking. The whole team works together through the progressive stages of production to lift the words from the script and create the images for the film story.

Here's a short list of the various jobs in the key creative categories:

- **Cinematography** — Director of photography, camera operator, focus puller, gaffer, clapper/loader, lamp operator, grip, video assist, digital imaging technician.
- **Production design** — Production designer, set designer, costume designer, illustrator, art director, graphic designer, painter, set decorator, prop master, make-up, hair, wardrobe, special effects make-up.
- **Post** — Picture editor, post-production supervisor, music supervisor, dialogue editor, sound designer, sound editor, colour correction technician, visual effects supervisor.
- **Sound** — location mixer, boom operator, studio sound technician, foley artist, sound designer, re-recording mixer.
- **Producing** — Producer, production manager, visual effects producer, production coordinator, location manager, production accountant, publicist, EPK producer.
- **Directing** — Director, assistant director, second unit director, casting director, script supervisor, storyboard artist, stunt coordinator, choreographer, dialect coach.
- **Writing** — Screenwriter, story editor, researcher.

There are many, many more jobs: film composer, stills photographer, animal wrangler, generator operator, location scout, construction coordinator, on-set carpenter, on-set painter, etc., etc., etc.

Not all employment opportunities in film are creative, nor do all require a formal education.

IT'S A MARATHON

The *third trick* is that the finish line for film school is the beginning of another marathon. Like every discipline, the highest achievers are always studying, always learning, always striving to be better.

A successful marathon is one that you complete. Winning or losing is secondary—it's the setting of the goal and realizing the accomplishment that are the important things. Finishing requires stamina, pacing and perseverance.

I've never run a marathon but I know many people who have. None of them just woke up one morning and said, 'I'm running a marathon today.' All of them trained, long and hard. Film school requires the same spirit of planning, effort and commitment.

Before you take another step, you should know what filmmaking entails and decide if a career in film is a lifestyle that appeals to you. The industry is demanding and competitive. You need to know what you're getting into—and you need to be ready for it.

The standard work week for television and film production starts at 60 hours and is often longer. Overtime is acknowledged on union shows but most schedules are built on the idea that everyone works a 12-hour shift. If you're commuting, add that time on to your day.

Most film jobs are temporary contracts. You are essentially a private contractor going from project to project. When you get a contract, you have to start thinking about the next one. Phone calls, networking and letting people know about your future availability are a standard part of the freelance film worker's routine.

If you're determined to advance in a field, you can set that goal in motion while you're in film school. Commit to the never-ending marathon and fill your days with film. Become the consummate 'filmmaker-in-training.'

Your goals may change as you advance in school and the industry. You discover new interests, develop new skills or realize new talents—things you never dreamed would happen before you started on your journey. Remember, the destination that one sets out for may not always be where they end up.

Trust that you will find the right path.

THE MAJOR DRAMATIC QUESTION

In The Courage to Teach, Parker J. Palmer writes, "To educate is to guide students on an inner journey toward more truthful ways of seeing and being in the world." This inner journey is vital for storytellers—and for anyone choosing to pursue an education in film.

Learning how to make a film means learning how to tell a story. The first thing a storyteller must know is the major dramatic question. This central organizing concept is key for the telling of a good tale: it provides the foundation and spine for the action. The major dramatic question usually states the main concern for the protagonist.

In the context here, *you* are the protagonist: the hero of the story.

Going to film school may prompt many questions, but start with the big one:

Why go to film school?

Answers I've heard:

"I just want to tell my stories."

"Great films and filmmakers inspire me."

"My dream is to work in the entertainment field."

Deciding that you are definitely going to film school is the first step of your journey. The next step is developing a realistic strategy for manifesting your best education: your best film school experience.

Your thoughts, ideas and opinions are important, and so is your productivity. You have to capture your ideas, develop your thoughts and shape your opinions. You have to secure them in words and images. That's what filmmaking is.

Film is art and making art requires effort. You have to do the work—and you have to show it. That's what filmmakers do.

Some of the activities in this book ask you to share your work and discuss your ideas with others. Feedback, analysis and critical thinking are going to be important for your learning experience. Always strive to find the constructive aspects of any criticism—both giving and receiving.

At the end of our time together, you'll have a cache of creative assets and a grasp of the soft skills that you'll need to make good films. You'll be ready to demonstrate your confidence and unleash your potential. When you get to film school, the work you put in here will be of significant value—starting on day one.

My first bit of advice: have some fun with it!

CREATIVE BINDER
FIRST DAY

I've had the privilege of meeting hundreds of students on their first day of film school. This opening class is their opportunity to make a good first impression. I ask everyone to introduce themselves and give a brief background. More importantly, I ask them why they're here and what they'd like to learn.

Surprisingly, many have not really thought about it. The general response is, 'I like to watch movies.'

People who like to watch films don't need to invest in a film education; people who make films do.

Going to film school is a big decision. Reasons can change, but it helps to establish a starting position.

YOUR FIRST ASSIGNMENT

WRITE A MISSION STATEMENT.

Communicate the reasons why you're at film school and what you hope to accomplish, in one or two sentences. Knowing your mission statement will be helpful on your first day.

. . . .

Start a creative binder to keep your thoughts, ideas, notes—and all of the exercises you do here.

. . . .

Note to self: Things change.

MY MISSION STATEMENT FOR PRIMER
To prepare students for a successful and creative education in film production, and inspire them to plan a winning strategy for life after film school.

PART II

STARTING OUT

Setting a vision that is bigger than what you've

previously set for yourself—and achieving

it—is how dreams turn into reality.

I didn't really discover any interest in film until I was a junior in college.

- GEORGE LUCAS

No, I never went to college. Always regretted it, always envied people who did.

- SYDNEY POLLACK

I had a terrible education. I attended a school for emotionally disturbed teachers.

- WOODY ALLEN

FILM SCHOOL FORMULA

[Talent + Goals] x Effort = Outcomes

This is the key for understanding the potential of your film school experience. How you apply yourself inside the academic timeframe is totally in your control. You determine your outcome.

TALENT

Talent happens. It's a gift, a natural ability, an aptitude. If you've got it, flaunt it. There's no downside in bringing your best to everything you do.

Yes, talent can be developed and improved. Still, no matter how long or hard you work at something, there are going to be times when other people perform better.

Artists compete, as do athletes, architects and chess players. Schools, cities and countries all engage in competitions to hand out trophies to winners. People challenge themselves to see how far they can push their talents. There is a natural inclination to improve, to better the outcome, to take it to the next level. Almost everyone competes.

Setting a vision that is bigger than what you've previously set for yourself—and achieving it—is how dreams turn into reality.

Consider your own talents and the ones that you want to develop. What are some of the things that you do well? Take the time to reflect on what you're good at, particularly the moments that are memorable because this helps you target your best outcomes.

Maybe you've had a surprising experience where you excelled. Maybe you created something, solved a problem or had a life-changing realization about your abilities, like shooting an arrow for the first time and hitting a bulls-eye. It might be a fluke. Or it might be a clue. Where it may lead, nobody knows.

It's these kinds of 'Aha moments' that have changed the course of people's lives, and the course of history. It can happen unexpectedly without prompting or anticipation: anywhere, anytime.

If it happens when you're doing something that you enjoy, then this might lead to something more: a life-long hobby, an invention, a career, or an award-winning film.

You have to be aware and take notice when special things happen: you need to recognize your gifts. If you're motivated to pursue and further develop a talent, this can make all the difference in your world.

Talents need to be demonstrated or they cannot be assessed. If you're in the creative arts, your ideas need to transform into something tangible, into what they are supposed to be, so that others can appreciate them. People want to hear your song, read your poem and gaze at your painting.

Making a film is a process of translating your ideas, in concert with your talents, into a physical form. In the motion picture industry, you need to show that you have what it takes to do the job. When you get an opportunity to step up and prove that you can handle a task—deliver your best.

CREATIVE BINDER
TALENTS & INTERESTS

EXAMPLES:

> *"I'm pretty good at telling jokes and people enjoy my humour. Film is exciting and I'm drawn to it. I'd like to write and direct comedies."*

Demonstrate that you can write a story. If it's a comedy, great! A well-written story is something you can share with others—like future classmates. It might become a screenplay, and maybe a film.

Or…

Make a short film. It doesn't have to be an epic. Have fun with it. Again, it's something you can share with classmates.

*"I love photography. I've been taking pictures
for a long time and people tell me that I've got
a good eye. I'd like to be a cinematographer."*

Organize a handful of your best photos. They might be landscapes, street scenes or portraits, but get them ready to show. There are schools that put an emphasis on photography in portfolios.

If a picture provokes a thousand words, let that be the filter for the images that you select. Ask yourself, "what is the story of this picture? What emotion does it capture? How does a viewer interpret and evaluate it?"

*"I'm athletic. I like stunts and action. Those
are the kinds of films that I want to make. I'm
interested in editing and visual effects."*

Write an action scene in screenplay format (more on this later.) Show that you can create a story event with dynamic characters and engaging dialogue.

Get your hands on a camera that shoots video, even if it's a smartphone, and put together a short action sequence that shows your skills at visual storytelling. If you can add visual effects, great!

Or...

Create the frame-by-frame drawings [storyboards] to show how you would piece together the necessary shots of a chase scene that you would like to direct.

IDENTIFY YOUR INTERESTS:

What do you like to read? What magazine articles grab your attention? What sections of the library or bookstore do you like to explore? What do you like to do in your free time? Make a long list.

CATALOGUE YOUR TALENTS:

Make a comprehensive list of each skill, ability and aptitude you can think of. Are you a whiz at solving the Rubik's cube? Do you have a good memory? How about something completely different, like juggling, hacky sack or baking pies. Nothing is too silly. The longer the list, the better.

ASK OTHERS ABOUT YOUR SKILLS:

People may see talents that you have overlooked. Their answers might surprise you. Write them all down.

CONTEMPLATE YOUR FILM-RELATED TALENTS.

For example, you may have an eye for detail, a flair for design or strong organizational skills. All of these are relevant in filmmaking. Which ones are you actively working on to develop? In what ways are you trying to improve your creative talents? If you were going to watch instructional videos, what would they be about?

REFINE YOUR CREATIVE TALENTS LIST.

Prioritize the talents that you are able to demonstrate in a portfolio. Note the ones that could support your academic goals. Focus on these key talents. Expand on them. Make them part of your extra-curricular activities.

. . . .

D.I.Y. TALENTS

I had never heard of 'foley' nor had any idea of what a 'foley artist' did before I went to film school.

What is foley? During the principal photography of a film, the sound recordist and boom operator focus on getting the best recording of the dialogue, the spoken words from the actors in the scene. Other sounds, like footsteps, squeaky doors, clothes rustle, etc. are added later—and this is called 'foley.'

What does a foley artist do? They work exclusively in post-production recreating most of the sounds that the audience hears when they see the action in a finished film. Once I realized the importance of sound design in creating and shaping the emotional impact of a scene, I was hooked.

I love performing foley. I've done it for three features that went on to screen at the top festivals in the world. No one ever 'taught' me how to do it. I learned out of necessity because I needed it for my own productions. I had a natural talent for it, went on to study and research it further, and got better at it. It's super creative, a lot of fun and an important aspect of the film viewer's experience.

The moral: in film school, you learn by doing. Keep your options open and never lose that do-it-yourself attitude.

GOALS

Consciously or unconsciously, you are setting and achieving goals every day. Different goals have different priorities and timelines. When you accomplish a noteworthy goal, it's important to acknowledge that you've done it. Celebrate your achievements! Each one helps you in your film school journey.

Setting goals and managing outcomes become easier as you gain more experience. Filmmaking requires you to accomplish goals in progressive stages: setting them, revising them and seeing them through to completion will be important pieces of your education puzzle.

Making a list is one way to keep your active goals in your attention zone on a daily basis. Mind mapping is also a popular strategy for creative thinkers. It's a brainstorming strategy, like a freewheeling flow chart that connects details, steps and stages without imposing a rigid structure. Visualizing how the various phases of a project link together can help you gain clarity.

Organization leads to greater productivity, better time management and stronger outcomes. Find organization tools that help you prioritize and strategize your goals—long term, short term, daily, personal, etc. Goals are the stepping-stones to a life well lived.

If you think you have what it takes to be a director—then you'll need to have a good script. The chances of a good script magically appearing in your hands is pretty slim. Most first-time film directors write their own, as do most students. If you want to direct, you can put **write a good script** at the top of your list of things you need to do.

There are common goals that all filmmakers share. Getting better at storytelling is vital if you want to advance in a creative role. Improving your story skills is more than a goal: it's an ongoing professional development requirement.

There's a practical acronym to apply to goal setting—and it's fitting for higher education: SMART.

S   is for Specific

M   is for Measurable

A   is for Attainable

R   is for Realistic

T   is for Time-bound

For example, if you want to get behind the camera and eventually work as a cinematographer, that is a **specific** goal—and a long-term one where you work your way up the industry ladder.

Let's say that you have no experience. You sign up for a program with hands-on training and get the chance to shoot a couple of films. That is a **measurable** change from where you started. You now have experience and could be hired as a trainee.

Is a cinematographer position **attainable**? Absolutely. You may have to move to a city that is a production hub, but opportunities abound. Commercials, music videos and television shows all need cinematographers.

Realistic? It can happen but you have to make it happen. Climbing the ladder of experience to get to the top job is literally a step-by-step process.

The schedule is the **time-bound** factor. If you start with no experience and two years later you have a demo reel to show producers or clients who might hire you, that would be a significant accomplishment in a set period of time.

If you plan on studying for a year or more at film school then you would be wise to embrace the next acronym (also the title of this section): GOALS.

G   is for Gainful Employment

O   is for Objective

A   is for Affordable

L   is for Logical

S   is for Strategy

Gainful employment is a term you'll hear if you engage with private or vocational schools in select countries. In the United States, for example, these schools have to adhere to regulations and standards established by the U.S. Department of Education, such as program completion rates, and job placement numbers (including typical income earnings) for their graduates.

Most students need to find employment soon after they graduate in order to repay loans and cover other expenses. Will you find a job? How long will it take before you get a pay cheque? What earning opportunities will be available to you after graduating? The answers to these questions are critical. That's why certain schools are required to disclose the gainful employment information of their graduates.

The film industry is notorious for exploiting newcomers with the opportunity of unpaid internships. These can be a great training ground and lead to even greater opportunities, but it is not gainful employment if you are not getting paid.

If your **objective** is to become a cinematographer for big-budget features, you'll need production education and lots of practical experience. Hands-on training to use the lights, cameras and grip equipment is a must. The film graduate's initial objective is to get a foot in the door in the camera or electrical departments. Any time you can be on set is another opportunity for practical experience and a chance to learn.

Is it **affordable?** If you are not skilled at estimating the likely costs of your education goals—get help. The downside of failing to understand the true costs of your education and the repayment of debt from student loans cannot be overstated.

Is it **logical?** Every student's journey is unique. What is logical for you depends on your personal situation. Are you physically able to hike to distant locations, climb ladders, and carry equipment? Are you good with shift work where you're shooting all night and sleeping all day? Would travel and being apart from your family be a problem? Only you know the answers.

Film production is a tree of specializations with many different branches. It takes a crew of actors, artists and technicians working together through demanding schedules to get a film project finished. You have to be prepared to do whatever it takes.

Your **strategy**—your plan to achieve your creative and academic goals—is probably the greatest deciding factor in your outcomes. Some choose a one-year training program and jump right into a job; some want a more fully-rounded education or a university degree; while others go on to post-graduate studies and advanced degrees.

Achieving your goals is about making choices, setting plans in motion, and following through. Film goals need to be refined and prioritized, otherwise, there can be setbacks, confusion, or worse—you might give up on your dreams.

SMART GOALS can help you form a winning strategy for your education plans, save you from making mistakes with your time and money, and keep your dreams alive.

CREATIVE BINDER
SMART GOALS

EXAMPLES:

> *"I'd like to start as an assistant in post-production*
> *and work my way up to be a picture editor.*
> *Eventually, I'd like to direct but I know that*
> *making that transition will take time."*

The hyphenate education, such as *editor-director*, or any combination of specializations, is an approach that I strongly recommend.

Select two specializations that you are interested in pursuing. Research people who have done both, someone who started as an editor and then moved up to directing. Watch their films. Find personal interviews. See what you can discover about their background and education. What was their first professional editing gig? When did they advance to directing?

"I want to write, direct and produce my own short film and submit it to festivals. Hopefully, I'll win an award and be able to kickstart a bigger project with some financial backing."

There are many stages and milestones involved with this goal, and you have to wear a lot of different hats. Writer/director/producer responsibilities require expertise in each role for the best chances of realizing a good film. Marketing your film and yourself are also going to be important, and these require separate skills that have their own fields of study and expertise.

Find films that you admire that are credited to a writer/producer/director. Research their first films, short films, and student films. Look into how the filmmaker works and study the films for cost, timeline and outcomes for the filmmaker. Note the marketing aspects of the films and the filmmaker.

"I just want to shoot films. I want to graduate with a demo reel, get a job on a camera team and start bringing in some money as soon as possible."

Focusing on one specialization and excelling in a key creative role still requires a thorough knowledge of the integration, workflow and team dynamics of film production.

Cinematographers tell stories with light and lenses. Understanding character development, narrative structure and the visual language of cinema will improve your opportunities to advance.

Make a list of the cinematographers that you admire. Read articles and interviews about their training, their movies and how they got to their position.

- **List** the goals you would like to achieve in your dream career. It may seem overwhelming, but take your time and think of them in milestones. Aim high.
- **Create** a list, roadmap or mind map of how and when you would ideally get to each progressive stage.
- **Share** your ideas with someone who knows you. The perspectives of a trusted friend can be invaluable.
- **Discuss** your ideas with an industry professional or a film educator. This is best to do with someone who has nothing to gain or lose from your decisions.
- **Refine** your education goals. Do the math. Crunch the numbers. How much will it cost? How long will it take? What's best for you?
- **Build** a timeline. Note the milestones and when you hope to accomplish them.
- **Write** it all down in as much detail as you can.
- **File** it in your creative binder.

Check back every six months or so to chart your progress. You might discover something along the way that you didn't anticipate: a talent, a skill or an interest. You may want to periodically update or redo this exercise.

. . . .

EFFORT

Effort is linked with enthusiasm and ability.

You've probably noticed that when you're having a good time and doing something you love, you experience a special flow of energy. In some cases, you lose track of time and keep working (or playing) long past your usual hours. These can be important signposts to note.

Creative projects, particularly films, take a lot of energy and effort to be finished to their potential. In order to stand out from the crowd in the world of film, you'll have to work hard, but you'll also need to 'work smart'. (this is different than *smart goals*.)

When you enjoy the work, you are 'working smart.' You're energized because you like what you're doing and you're interested in the outcome. You want to do your best, finish strong, and be proud of the work. Conversely, when you're uncertain or stressed out, you can find yourself in a desperate struggle to come up with ideas or solutions. For many, the stress of being creative on a deadline is new and challenging territory to navigate. Especially when the schedules are tight.

Assessing the potential of any assignment is important for managing the time and energy that you put towards it. A golden opportunity is something that you don't want to miss. How you plan, approach and finish a project can be a game-changer. Always think ahead of the curve and consider how any project might move you toward your goals in life after film school.

I want to share an inspirational story about a student who put in a tremendous effort on his first film assignment in a one-year program. This initial project was an opportunity to write, produce, direct and edit your own film; in subsequent productions, you'd work in creative teams and specialize in one production role.

Ben C. had done some visual effects self-education before coming into the program. It made sense for him to do a project where he could build on his talents and abilities. He pitched a story that worked for the constraints of the assignment: one-actor, one-location, and a one-day shoot.

His project was meticulously planned. The footage was shot in ten hours and then crafted through ten weeks of post-production. He logged over 250 hours in picture editing, sound design and visual effects while still attending full-time classes and completing other homework.

Ben made a commitment and finished his film on time for the screening deadline. He presented his no-budget, science-fiction short and got an enthusiastic response from the audience. I've since screened Ben's film for hundreds of students on their first day of school as an example of what *can* be done.

Ben graduated and went straight into a visual effects position at a video game company, quickly establishing himself as a key creative collaborator.

Doing your best work and getting it in front of the people who can take your talents to the next level is the path to success in the creative industries.

Film school won't change your work ethic.
It will define it.

MATH AND FILM

First-year math was a struggle. I just couldn't wrap my head around the concepts of statistics or remember the formulas for probability. It seemed like a huge waste of time; something that I would never use; and on top of it all—I didn't enjoy it.

At the final exam, I drew a total blank on the first few questions. I didn't know how or where to start. Things got progressively worse as the minutes ticked by. I became more and more frustrated. It was mental torture.

There was no value in just guessing but I knew I had to do something. So, instead of providing numerical answers, I challenged the questions as being abstract and too broad. I wrote short responses to each problem arguing why there could be no valid answer.

Long story short—I got a zero. This lowered my GPA considerably and jeopardized my chances of getting into the film program.

In the admission interview, the head of the department noted the grade and asked me about it. I told her that I had indeed failed that course. I recounted my final exam story in the most compelling fashion, throwing in some sample questions and my profound responses.

"That's a funny story," she said with a smile. "We're not looking for math-types around here."

Two weeks later, I got my letter. I was in!

Looking back on my failure in math, it's not that I didn't work hard. Quite the contrary, I worked very hard. I even signed up for extra-tutorial sessions. Here's the thing: I didn't get any joy out of answering math problems—and there was no end to them! If you figured one out, they'd give you five more. I never had a sense of accomplishment.

Failing math put my academic standing in peril. But fortunately, with a little storytelling on short notice, it actually helped me get into the film program. What is the probability of that?

OUTCOMES

There are many filmmakers throughout history who set ambitious goals for their student productions. Two notable examples are George Lucas and Francis Ford Coppola, trailblazers and legends, both at school and in their professional careers. While enrolled at university, they made memorable films at the opposite ends of the filmmaking spectrum: Lucas did a 60 second short and Coppola finished a 97-minute feature.

Lucas went to the University of Southern California (USC) but not to study film, initially. He discovered his interest in filmmaking through an animation course. The term project required students to shoot one-minute of film, 1440 frames, using the school animation equipment. This was an exercise to demonstrate that they understood the camera and frame-by-frame creation of movement.

While others were happy to do pencil drawings of a bouncing ball, Lucas created a photo montage from magazine clippings with a vision beyond the silent frames. His film told a story using a stylized collage of images. He later added sound, music and narration.

Lucas worked within the guidelines and constraints of the assignment but took a completely original and creative approach. His film was experimental, but narrative; abstract, yet grounded in the zeitgeist of the 1960s. It engaged the audience and made them feel something.

The difference between George Lucas and every other student is that his class assignment went to festivals around the world. It even has a Wikipedia page: *Look at Life*.

Coppola, on the other hand, won a playwriting scholarship while he was pursuing a major in theatre arts at college. He graduated, gained experience in the professional film business, and went back to school enrolling at the University of California Los Angeles (UCLA) graduate film program. He set out to do something no one else had done before: shoot a feature film for his thesis project.

You're a Big Boy Now (1966) got a theatrical release, some critical acclaim and put Coppola on the radar as a director.

Lucas and Coppola set their own standards. They approached their assignments with an eye to creating something bold, something different. They demonstrated their inventive spirit in school and went on to break new ground as pioneers in the film industry.

The outcome of every project is the summation of your talents, goals, and efforts. If you know the outcome you want to achieve, **do the math**.

BIG IDEAS

In my directing courses, students work through script analysis, scene study and various techniques to help them visually construct their stories. The term project is an original short scene to be written, shot and completed as homework outside of class time.

I once had a student who was doing well in class and actively participated in all of the workshops. When I would check in and ask if everyone was moving ahead with their projects, he'd always smile and nod. He never asked for help or gave any indication that he was struggling.

On screening day, he showed up empty-handed. I was disappointed because it meant he would fail the course. Afterwards, I asked what had happened to cause him to miss the deadline.

"My ideas are too big," he said.

"But everything we worked on was about little ideas," I replied. He nodded and shrugged.

Everything starts with the little pieces: truthful moments captured in beautiful frames that tell your story. Scenes are about creating emotion, examining behaviour and exploring the human experience.

Bigger stories are just a collection of short scenes built from moments that weave together.

Sadly, he dropped out of the program.

THREE BIG QUESTIONS

Imagine that you have an original idea that you think would make a great film. You follow your passion and shape your idea into a compelling story. You write it as a screenplay. People like it.

You create a plan to bring it to life as a film. Maybe you produce. Maybe you direct.

It's not a matter of who is going to let you do it, but rather, who is going to stop you.

Ultimately—you make your film. It's a hit! It plays at festivals around the world. It launches your career.

This is the dream. Many have lived it. But not all of them went to film school. This fact has prompted a long-standing debate on the necessity of film education, particularly for the digital learner in the digital age.

The issue of whether going to film school is the right choice for a particular individual creates more questions than answers.

Here are three connected questions that can refine your ideas and help you move forward with your decision:

> Do I need to go to film school?
>
> Do I need to go to a particular film school?
>
> Do I need to go to a particular film school now?

DO I NEED TO GO TO FILM SCHOOL?

We can't go further without addressing the elephant in the room. If you Google this question, more than 30 million results come up. You'll find plenty of commentaries, but this chapter is about refining the answers that are right for you. This is a pivotal fork in the road, and my advice here is to slow down, take a thorough look at the details and review your options.

The goal of a film education is different for everyone. Some want to come away with technical skills; some want to make a 'calling card' film; some want the degree—and the marks—to continue on to a higher level of education.

It's important to know what you plan to do with your education and how you believe it can benefit you. There are eight creative areas of specialized study to consider and they each have unique dynamics and skill sets:

1.) Writing
2.) Directing
3.) Producing
4.) Production Design*
5.) Location Sound Mixing
6.) Editing
7.) Cinematography
8.) Post-Production Sound

*Hair, Make-up, and Wardrobe are important jobs on film sets. There are schools that focus directly on these specializations. Pursuing a career in these areas does not require a film production education.

Different programs provide varying degrees of training and emphasis on film production specializations. Not everyone who goes to film school wants to pursue a career as a producer, a production designer, or a location sound mixer. However, you should understand the responsibilities and challenges of every department in the filmmaking chain. The best way to learn is to do them all—at least once.

By going to film school, you can gain hours of production experience in every area by helping your classmates with their films. That's the design of most programs. There can also be opportunities to take on roles in productions being done in other classes.

In addition to technical training and production experience on other films, you also have a cohort of classmates to help you make yours. One of the upsides of film school is the community you develop and the friends you make. Being around people with similar interests and common goals can set the foundation for shared success after graduation. There are countless examples of people who continued working together after meeting in film school.

If you want to make a film alone, it can be done. Animation and stop-motion are fields where students can work independently. But most live-action films are the result of collaboration and teamwork.

Working in production teams is one of the ways that a film program differs from other faculties. Learning to collaborate, delegate and manage a creative team are important aspects of any film education. Soft skills, such as creative problem solving, knowing how to get along with people, leadership abilities, etc. are valuable attributes in the industry. More on this later.

CREATIVE BINDER
SCHOOL CRITERIA

Primary categories for evaluating a film school:

1.) Cost - the determining factor for many;

2.) Status - schools earn their reputations;

3.) Faculty - your partners in education;

4.) Location - if you're relocating, that's a big deal;

5.) Curriculum & Production - the learning engine;

6.) Equipment & Facilities – the filmmaking essentials;

Additional aspects that should not be overlooked:

7.) Class size - bigger is not better;

8.) Environment & culture - creativity needs support;

9.) Transferable credits – not a guarantee, acceptance depends on the destination school;

10.) Copyright - owning the work you produce;

11.) Internships, practicums & placements – can be the icing on the cake of a good education.

Note the ones that are important to you.

Order them in a priority sequence.

Create a spreadsheet, chart or table to organize the information that you gather about specific schools. This will be helpful in analyzing and comparing your program options.

. . . .

DO I NEED TO GO TO A PARTICULAR FILM SCHOOL?

There are many different types of schools to consider. The education you receive and the films you make will depend, primarily, on the program you choose.

The landscape of film education is vast and ever-changing. You'll learn different things in different ways from different teachers. It's important to realize that there are no standard prerequisites and no standard outcomes.

All schools provide varying levels of basic technical training. Some programs focus on dramatic narrative film, others lean towards experimental or documentary. You can find schools for specialized technical training; general diploma and certificate programs; and advanced graduate programs for a Masters of Fine Arts (MFA) degree.

Film schools are ranked annually by different sources including the Hollywood Reporter and Variety. These lists incorporate perspectives from industry insiders, filmmakers and film school grads rating programs based on categories such as cost, facilities, faculty, student evaluations, and alumni success.

Some schools are consistently ranked among the top in the world. For example, USC has earned its reputation for their alumni, faculty, extensive resources, and industry access.

Graduating from a reputable film school can have a positive impact on how you're initially regarded in the industry. If only the best will do, a school's ranking on these lists might be one of your priority considerations.

Top-ranked schools have a demanding admissions process and lofty tuition fees. There is also plenty of competition for seats. USC recently had over 4,800 would-be students applying for fewer than 300 slots. This is one reason why some students start working on their post-secondary goals early on in high school.

Admission starts as a numbers game on both sides: students apply to several schools, schools get more applications than they can realistically review. In order to make the process manageable, applications are initially filtered by grades. If your marks are good, you move on to the next round and another qualifying filter. However, it's a different situation if the program is undersubscribed. Some schools are set up as private companies in the business of film education. Their only source of income is from tuition fees. Therefore, they advertise, recruit and sign up every student they can.

If you're looking for hands-on technical training with the latest tools, you need to know the kind of equipment and facilities that the school has. Creating an impressive demo reel requires up-to-date gear in good working condition. You also need to have reasonable access to it. Sometimes a school may have great camera equipment, but unless you're in the right class or have passed the right training you may not be able to use it. Rules and restrictions for equipment use are important to know up front.

Higher education in the arts is about immersing yourself in a creative environment and integrating with a peer group of like-minded individuals. Film nights and extra-curricular activities all help to build and maintain a connected student body.

Relationships with classmates can resonate long after classes have ended. Championing their projects, appreciating their talents and making a constructive contribution to a creative team might prove to be the most important and marketable aspect of your education.

Film production students learn in small groups and crews. The team education model is standard across most film production programs. A student film crew is a scaled-down version of a working industry production.

This team dynamic can be one of the key strengths of a program. It's also one of the key challenges. A film class that shows a good balance of interests across the different specializations is the best-case-scenario. However, achieving this balance is difficult. The problem is that the selection of classmates who are with you for the length of the program is basically out of your hands.

You can find online forums dedicated to reviews of film schools. Do your due diligence on researching the accuracy of these sources as some can be years out of date. To find current perspectives about a particular school, try to initiate discussions with students who are already enrolled. Students have a strong sense of community. It's important to hear about other student experiences.

I strongly recommend that you go the extra mile when evaluating your top choices. Look and compare with what other schools have to offer. The highest-ranked program in the world doesn't mean it's the best one for you.

While the elite schools may provide you with a valuable credential in the job market, the quality of the student experience is equally, if not more, important.

CREATIVE BINDER
SCHOOL SELECTION

EXAMPLES:

"I'm interested in a school environment that feels comfortable and creative. I'm not sure that a short, intense program fits with the way that I like to learn."

Students who are currently enrolled at a school, or recent graduates, are your best resource for information about the program. You can sleuth online but watch for outdated or anonymous posts.

Events, activities, theme nights and film series are good opportunities to meet other students and grow your creative community.

If there are schools in your vicinity, attend an extra-curricular event that has a creative focus. Check out a play, an art showing or a student film presentation. This will give you an idea for the level of the work and the student demographic.

> *"What's most important for me is the faculty. I have a bit of experience in filmmaking and I'm going back to school specifically to make a film. I want to be encouraged and challenged. I want teachers who can inspire me."*

Auditing classes or sitting in for a lecture is a good use of time if you're shopping for a school. If you have a bit of filmmaking background, this can help you gain a greater understanding of the program.

Being curious is an excellent attribute for filmmakers to develop. Google everyone. Who is the head of the program? Who are the full-time teachers? What is their background? Who will be teaching you?

Don't be misled by an impressive list of adjuncts who may have taught there in the past, there is no guarantee that you will ever see them. Furthermore, the likelihood that adjuncts or any part-time professors have made a significant contribution to the program content or curriculum design is remote.

Some schools advertise that you'll be learning from 'industry professionals.' While this sounds assuring, it's been a source of frustration for many students. Teaching is a profession that requires training, skills and commitment. Professional filmmakers are not necessarily good teachers.

You want teachers who are going to show up prepared to present engaging material with strong learning outcomes and have a through-line with your best educational interests in mind.

> *"I'm looking for a program where I can explore my creative voice."*

The curriculum is the contract between the school and the student. Course descriptions are helpful, so the more information you have on specific content, the better position you'll be in to make a decision that's right for you. You'll also be in a better position to prepare for your education if you know what you're going to be learning and some of the books that are recommended.

Workshops are important for practical hands-on training. In order to be effective, they need focus and structure. What workshops are offered? What is the class size of the workshops? What are the learning outcomes?

Schools have equipment and facilities, but it's important to find out how many films each student makes on average in the program. What are the limitations on the projects? Where can you see some of the films that students have made? Can the school arrange for you to connect with recent graduates?

BEYOND THE
OPEN HOUSE

Most schools open their doors at least once a year to offer prospective students a chance to look around the campus. They bring out equipment, screen films made in the program, and have teachers, staff and student representatives available to answer questions.

There is plenty to learn from attending these affairs. And more can be learned if you explore beyond the open house:

Audit a lecture or workshop to get an idea of class size, student demographics and curriculum delivery;

Sit in on a test screening or film critique. Hear feedback on student work in progress;

Engage with students in the halls, cafeteria, or library. This can be an eye-opener. Start with something like, 'Hi, I'm thinking of coming to the film program. Do you have a minute to tell me about it?' As you work through this book, keep track of specific questions that you'd like to have answered.

DO I NEED TO GO TO A PARTICULAR FILM SCHOOL NOW?

There are currently more than 1200 film schools in over 80 countries. They have sprung up on an average of one per month since the Soviet Academy first opened its doors in 1919. This growth trend shows no signs of changing anytime soon.

If you really, really, really have to go to film school—you most definitely can. You could be starting class in a couple of months. There are hundreds of programs that will accept you—sight unseen. All you need to do is fill out an application, answer a skill-testing question, pay the fees, and BOOM! You're in film school.

The allure of filmmaking is powerful. It stirs up strong urges and deep emotions. A good film education is a wonderful thing; a bad one can be ruinous and leave you in a worse place than where you started.

For higher education to be a positive, memorable milestone, be sure it fits with your budget, lifestyle and academic performance.

Level of maturity is also an important consideration. Some schools attract older, more experienced students. It can be difficult for anyone going straight from high school into a film production program where the average age is around 25 or 28, particularly because of the team learning approach and the politics of crewing up for production.

THE REBOUND
DILEMMA

Let's say that you apply to five reputable schools but don't get accepted to any of them. You seek a quick-fix solution, so you reset your sights to find a school that *will* accept you. And you do.

In fact, it was easy.

Their website looks great; the phone recruiters say it's awesome, and; you are the perfect student.

You pay your money, show up and soon discover that it's not the right fit. It happens.

You need to be careful about making a rebound choice for film education. If you think you're at the wrong school at the wrong time with the wrong people, you need to take action—even if it means taking a loss.

Making the most out of your education investment is the point of this book: you want to be at the right school for the right reasons.

But what if the school you want to go to is the one you can't get into? This happened to Steven Spielberg. He set out to study at USC but was rejected numerous times. He finally opted for another school, got in, realized it was the wrong fit and dropped out. Luckily, things worked out for him.

YOUR FILM SCHOOL BUDGET

Film and Fine Art degrees are among the most expensive in the world with some universities charging tuition fees that exceed $200,000 (USD) for a bachelor's degree. There are private schools that offer seats in a one-year program for over $50,000. On top of the fees, you have to factor in the additional costs of living expenses.

Film schools are not a case of 'you get what you pay for.' There are no guarantees. You are making an important investment of your time and money—plus the additional psychic energy of your dreams, hopes and creativity.

Education is a business: you are the customer. Don't shy away from the task of doing the budget. Crunch the numbers, get into the details, just like you would if you were making a film. Do your cost comparisons, read consumer reviews. The more informed you are, the better decisions you'll make.

BIG INVESTMENTS

A formal post-secondary education is a financial commitment. It requires you to enter into a legal contract to pay for services from an institute of higher learning: there is a myriad of details to consider.

61

Schools have a personality. Like first impressions, things aren't always evident at the outset. Once you're enrolled, you may discover details that you wish you'd learned about earlier.

Going to film school is like producing a film: your budget is critically important—it impacts everything. The more information you have, the more accurate you can be with your bottom-line.

If you have previous experience with higher education and budgeting or know someone who does, this will come in handy. Some banks offer student services and features that you can take advantage of, like a student budget calculator to estimate how much money you'll need per month.

Before you sign on the dotted line, you should clearly understand the fine print and the total cost of completing the program. You should know what you're buying, and your responsibilities as a student.

Top-ranked brands command top dollar. Money is a pivotal factor for most students and many rule out colleges based on sticker price alone.

Even if you have the cash on hand, I recommend exhausting all possibilities for financing. After all, if you're planning to invest thousands of dollars and years of your life, it's worth spending a few weeks researching possible sources of funding rather than draining your savings or racking up student loans.

Every story has stakes: the higher they are, the greater the dramatic tension. The stakes for you as a film student are more than financial. The choices you make and the risks you take are what will make your story unique.

Education should be an adventure, not a gamble. It should open up your mind and fill you with a sense of awe and wonder. Some people jump in with youthful impatience which can be exciting or frustrating depending on how, where and when you land.

Tuition fees are like movie budgets.
Just because it's a whole lot of money,
doesn't mean it's going to be good.

CREATIVE BINDER
FINANCING & COSTS

"Do I qualify for a scholarship, or is there any possibility of getting an educational grant?"

Research the grants, bursaries and scholarships that are affiliated with the school. This can be done through their financial aid offices. They don't hand them out. You need to inquire and apply. There will be qualifying factors, requirements and deadlines to meet. There can be various categories, such as need-based or merit-based grants.

Research scholarship databases online for a wider range of aid, including federal support or private sector funds. There can be restrictions on how scholarship money is spent. You must also be aware that any additional monies you receive may result in reductions to other aid or loan packages.

"Does the school provide support?"

Ask about financial support for student projects. If money is available, clarify the conditions that apply. Rules and policies vary. Sometimes students compete for funding or awards. Generally speaking, don't count on the school financing your films, so include a budget line item for creative work and make adjustments as you gather more information.

Ask about equipment support. The school may stipulate that students need to complete certain courses before using expensive gear, particularly cameras. Loss and damage deposits may also be required. Availability, accessibility and costs associated with using school equipment or facilities are good to know ahead of time.

"What is the estimated budget for
student films in the program?"

Request information on the estimated cost for student productions. These are details that the school should be able to provide up front.

Working with a cost per day is a good starting point for a budget. If the school is providing all of the necessary equipment, setting a budget of $300 to $500 per day is a reasonable guesstimate for a small crew (six or so people) plus two unpaid actors shooting in the daytime at a free location. A portion of your budget usually goes towards coffee, snacks and feeding your crew. Transportation and parking expenses all contribute to the final budget.

Costs would then scale up or down depending on the scope of the project. For example, a story of two injured soldiers separated from their regiment might have additional costs for uniforms, props, special effects or special effects makeup.

. . . .

COSTLY MISTAKES

Borrowing money is serious business. Education and training will arm you with knowledge and skills but it can also leave you with unmanageable debt.

Tuition prices and living expenses for today's students have increased significantly. Relocating for school or pursuing international studies can send costs soaring. Graduating with too much debt can be a burden that grows heavier every year. Debt is linked with interest costs and repayment schedules. Debt is also linked to stress and illness.

If you're like most students, higher education means taking out a student loan *and* losing potential income for the duration of the program. You need to evaluate how the cost and time of film school will impact your future goals and plans.

When it comes to financing your education, you want to be aware of the potential problems so that you can dodge them and avoid disappointments. If your budget requires you to have a part-time job while you're going to school, you need to have a clear understanding of how this will affect your education. What you don't want to happen is to fall short on funds or take on unanticipated debt partway through.

Some schools recommend that your best student experience means putting your education first and not taking on a part-time job while attending their program. If it's not possible for you to attend school without working you should factor that into your plans and school choice.

Volunteering on student films gives you the hands-on experience that you need for working in the industry. A part-time job on the weekend means that you won't be available and that's when you're most likely to be shooting in film school. If you can't make it to a weekend shoot because of your job, you are the one losing out on the experience and training.

KNOW YOUR
REFUND POLICY

If you arrive at school and get the feeling that it's just not the right fit, for whatever reason, you may have a week or two to opt out and still get a full, or near-full, reimbursement. You have to act fast though: refund windows are generally short.

Schools post a schedule for course changes and refunds. It's important to know these dates. At a certain point, usually several weeks along, you are all in. If you decide to change your mind after the refund window has closed, you'll owe the full fare. If you have a student loan, you'll be making payments on the full amount, plus interest, until the debt is cleared.

There are guidelines for student loans. You should seek the advice of someone who specializes in them. Don't borrow without knowing the rules.

This section is about making the right decisions and starting off on the right foot. There are not many major life investments that offer a money-back deal if you change your mind after buying a ticket and getting on board.

Trust your instincts. Refund windows are there for the benefit of students.

FASTER, BETTER, CHEAPER

The trend for digital filmmaking is towards shorter production schedules and tighter deadlines. Driving creative projects at breakneck speed is best left in the hands of experienced filmmakers.

Making good films and telling memorable stories requires patience, skill and many layers of talent.

Rushing through any stage of film school or the learning process is contrary to the purpose of making art; making good art requires contemplation.

Vocational training on industry equipment can prepare you for entry-level technical and support positions. It's considerably more difficult to land a job in a lead creative role when you are right out of school. Directing, cinematography, editing, design and producing jobs are coveted positions. In most cases, you have to create your own opportunities or work your way up the experience ladder just to earn the consideration for an interview.

Anyone taking on a role with creative responsibilities needs to draw on their knowledge, experience and talent to deliver on their duties and manage their teams. There is no fast-track to the top jobs in film.

FILMMAKING AND EDUCATION
If it's exceptionally organized—it can be faster.
If it's thoroughly prepared—it can be better.
If it's meticulously planned—it can be cheaper.

PART III

Films are like finished jigsaw puzzle pictures:

close scrutiny reveals the intricate pieces

and shows you how it all fits together.

We welcome applications from motivated,
independent and hardworking individuals.
Students are in class 6-8 hours per day and
are also busy with homework, shooting and
writing scripts. During production periods,
which constitute 20-30 days per semester,
shooting may last up to 12-14 hours/daily.
Studies are very intensive and demanding,
and require a high level of personal discipline.

— EUROPEAN FILM SCHOOL WEBSITE

Things rarely happen overnight.
Filmmakers should be prepared for
many years of hard work. The sheer toil
can be healthy and exhilarating.

— WERNER HERZOG

ADVANCE SCHEDULE

Before the camera rolls or the director calls "ACTION!" there is a critically important stage in the filmmaking process called **pre-production.** This is the advance planning phase for organizing, gathering and preparing everything that's needed to make the film.

A well-organized plan with a detailed pre-production schedule gives you a better chance for success as a filmmaker *and* a film student. The amount of lead-time you have and how you use it is going to make a difference.

When you're a full-time film student, you are busy—very busy if you're doing it right. In addition to writing, studying and making films, you're also attending lectures and workshops while managing creative projects, term papers and exams. It's a high-wire juggling act that demands your ongoing concentration.

If you want to get ahead and stay ahead, use the time leading up to your arrival on campus as a designated development period: a chance to charge your creative batteries. Everything that you can do before showing up at school will pay off in the program.

In his book, *The Seven Habits of Highly Effective People,* Stephen R. Covey suggests to "begin with the end in mind." This is an excellent philosophy to embrace for film production, as well as education. If you make the effort to design a workable game plan for your film school experience, great things can be accomplished.

The purpose of film education is to position you for a creative role, a key technical job or facilitate your advancement as a filmmaker. There is every possibility that the projects you undertake in school can serve to single you out for an opportunity that you otherwise might never have had.

A well-written script, an impressive demo reel, a thoughtful short film: these are a few examples of what you may be capable of completing through your education. Ideally, you graduate with a diploma in one hand and your best creative work in the other. To help make this a reality, the 21st century film student begins well before the first day of school.

CREATIVE BINDER
ADVANCE CALENDAR

Going to film school is like going to the gym: you are there to build muscles—creative ones. It's going to take time and dedication. You need to pace yourself, build your stamina and develop your technique. It's a process of growth and discovery.

Whether you have two months, ten months or longer—the time that you devote to raising your level of film knowledge contributes to the foundation that you build upon in school.

Time management and project planning are also fundamental skills to nurture. They are important in many aspects of filmmaking. Like most things, you learn them by doing them.

MAKE AN ADVANCE HOMEWORK CALENDAR.

In the months leading up to film school, plan on putting in a time commitment of 20 - 25 hours per week, or more. When you're in school you'll be putting in 25 hours on the weekend!

This book will provide you with ideas, exercises and strategies to help organize a feasible preliminary schedule. Finding the time and following through requires action on your part.

REFINE YOUR INTERESTS.

Start a new section in your binder for films, genres, themes, directors or actors that you're interested in. Use this as a starting point to lead you to the books, films and screenplays that will help you dig deeper and discover more. Research should lead you in new directions.

Take it one day at a time—starting now.

. . . .

BOOKS TO READ

There will be reading: many hours of reading. Find a comfortable chair and get ready to settle in with a few good books.

There's a wealth of information available. Every specialization has seminal books written by experts in their field. Research, reading and studying will make you a better filmmaker and a more valuable team member on any film crew.

Insights from directors, cinematographers and editors through decades of filmmaking are invaluable. Learning about the right and wrong choices of those who have gone before can help you avoid making the same mistakes.

There are recommended books and suggested reading lists for most courses in film schools. If you can get a list from your school and read them before your first day, that is the ideal scenario. You'll be that much further ahead on day one.

Here is my starter list for 'must read' books:

The 5 C's of Cinematography: Motion Picture Filming Techniques
By Joseph Mascelli

There's more to cinematography than just pretty pictures. Films are constructed as a chain of images that create the cinematic illusion of reality and lead the viewer through a compelling story.

Many students find it hard to remember what the '5 C's' stand for, and they draw a blank when I ask about the '6th C' (which is very important but only mentioned in the preface. Once students hear it, it's the one they never forget!).

The building blocks of filmmaking and image construction are all here. This is cinematography 101, and more. If you read it closely, you'll be more prepared to go out and start shooting a film.

Hitchcock Truffaut: A Definitive Study of Alfred Hitchcock
By Francois Truffaut, Alfred Hitchcock

Two master filmmakers from different backgrounds sit down for an in-depth discussion on film, directing, storytelling and the stuff of great cinema. They cover Hitchcock's body of work so you'll need to factor in additional time to watch the films: the films are critical for context.

The book is also the subject of a movie which has entertaining interviews and comments by filmmaking giants, such as Martin Scorsese, David Fincher, Wes Anderson, Richard Linklater, and more. Reading the book is invaluable—and something to enjoy many times over. It has inspired prominent directors and it will inspire you, too.

In the Blink of an Eye:
A Perspective on Film Editing
By Walter Murch

I'm a big fan of Walter Murch. He's a film editor, sound designer and a significant figure in the world of film. He's won Academy Awards for classics such as *The English Patient* and *Apocalypse Now.* He's also the subject of many articles and books for his innovation and influence in filmmaking.

Like Hitchcock, Murch considers the emotions of the story, as conveyed by the images and performances, to be the main storytelling priority for filmmakers.

A thorough understanding of the craft of editing will help you make strong choices at every stage of the filmmaking process.

George Lucas's Blockbusting: A Decade-by-Decade Survey of Timeless Movies Including Untold Secrets of Their Financial and Cultural Success
By Alex Ben Block, Lucy Autrey Wilson

A readable reference book from the creator of Star Wars with over 900 pages of gold: a treasure trove of valuable info. Excellent for research, organized decade by decade. It delves into the cultural, economic and business aspects of 300+ films.

This is comfy chair material. Something to open up and flip through for a better understanding of film history, trends, genres, technology, audience and the business of film.

Lucas didn't write this book, he commissioned it. As he states in the introduction: this is the book he wishes he could have had in film school. That's good enough for me.

Film Directing Fundamentals: See Your Film Before Shooting
By Nicholas Proferes

I use this book to teach directing and visual storytelling. It covers basic techniques as well as advanced concepts, such as film time, compression, elaboration, and more.

There's a sample script with a breakdown of how you develop it and think it through to a visual story—complete with floor diagrams and storyboards. There are lots of useful ideas that you can apply to your own short films. Important reading for the novice filmmaker.

CREATIVE BINDER
'MUST READ' BOOKS

1.) **Choose** a specialization that interests you. Google it '+ *books*'. For example: film producing + books, or film directing + books.

2.) **List** the books that grab your attention.

3.) **Read** the reviews. Take a look inside.

4.) **Check** at the library before you buy them.

5.) **Read actively.** Use post-it notes as tabs on pages that you want to refer back to.

6.) **Create** a blank bookmark from card paper, three or four inches wide. Use this to keep your place and jot down key points and page numbers. You can have more than one bookmark per book. Keep these bookmarks for future reference. They will come in handy.

SCREENPLAYS TO STUDY

Reading screenplays will help you write them, understand them, and turn them into films. You will be working with screenplays in film school. At some point, you will more than likely need to write one. The more exposure you have to the specific format that screenplays adhere to, the better prepared you'll be.

Screenwriting is a craft with strict industry guidelines. Writers use a stylistic template known as 'master scene format' which facilitates the production of the film through various stages. The format has been the accepted industry standard for decades.

Not everyone who goes to film school wants to write screenplays, but it's everyone's job to know how screenplays work and why they are written as they are. Lifting the words off the page and turning them into a flow of images and sounds is the job of the creative team. Everyone has to know how to read a screenplay.

Screenwriters follow the standard layout by using specialized software which makes the formatting easier with tabs for scene headings, descriptive paragraphs, dialogue, transitions, etc. A properly formatted script becomes the blueprint for the filmmaking team. It enables the detailed organization, scheduling and budgeting for efficient production.

Reading the screenplays of your favourite films gives you further insight into how words on the page transform into images and sounds. Studying the work of great screen-writers can help you develop your own voice as a storyteller in film.

Reading scripts and then watching the films gives you a behind-the-scenes glimpse into the crafts of directing, cinematography and every specialization. Going from script to screen is a process of interpretation. There is much to learn from reviewing the choices made by other filmmakers.

Screenplays for popular films can be found online. Be aware that sometimes you find a screenplay that has been created from the finished film. It may look like a production screenplay, but it might be a verbatim transcription of the released film or just the dialogue. This will be radically different from what the screenwriter initially wrote. It may bear no resemblance to the script that the director and production team used to create the film. For our purposes, you want to have the final shooting script. There may be multiple previous drafts, but I recommend checking the date on the cover page and finding the script the filmmaking team used to prep and shoot the film.

A good screenplay describes the action and keeps it visual. Writers use different techniques to guide the reader's eye and build mental images. You will quickly note the hallmarks of good screenwriting: concise language, minimal camera direction and a writerly style that supports the pacing and content.

Screenplays are written in the present tense with an understanding that the audience must be able to see or hear all of the details that are key to the story.

It should take about the same amount of time to read the script as it would to watch the film. The accepted industry calculation is one page per minute—90 pages would take

90 minutes—and the finished film probably runs about 90 minutes, too.

Everyone in a creative role needs to read, analyze and interpret screenplays. Actors, directors, producers, cinematographers, editors and designers all need to apply their specific skills and talents to bring the written words onto the screen.

The more screenplays you read and the more you familiarize yourself with the interpretive process of going from script to screen, the more confidence you'll have with making your own films.

CREATIVE BINDER
FROM SCRIPT TO SCREEN

1.) **Select** a film that made an impact on you, perhaps one that you've seen many times;

2.) **Source** the screenplay—final shooting draft, if possible;

3.) **Read** it closely, straight through in one sitting;

4.) **Screen** the film and **read along** with the screenplay in hand as you watch it;

5.) **Track** the significant changes;

6.) **Stop, go and rewind**, as necessary. *

*Note: The script rarely matches the finished film. Scenes, as written, may move or drop; dialogue will change; the ending may be different. This is part of the filmmaking process.

THE CONVERSATION (COPPOLA, 1974)

Francis Ford Coppola's *The Conversation* won the Palme d'Or at Cannes—the top prize at the top festival. It was a film that captivated me right from the opening shot.

Years later, I stumbled across the final production script and decided to read it straight through. The story was very different from the story that I remembered in the film. The characters were the same but the script was not even close to the movie in my memory, though I hadn't seen it in years.

I watched the film again with the script in hand. This was the first time I tried doing this.

I read along, often losing my place. It was profoundly confusing, but my memory served me well—the movie was nothing like the screenplay. Important scenes, plus an entire B story, had been dropped and completely cut out of the film.

Wow! Even the great ones like Coppola don't get it right, I thought. Rather than going from script to screen, this felt more like throwing the map away and hoping to find hidden treasure. I imagined that he just trusted that there's a better film to be found in the footage.

CUT TO: 18 years later, I read Michael Ondaatje's book, The Conversations—Walter Murch and the Art of Editing Film (2002 Vintage Canada Edition.) I stopped dead in my tracks (on page 157) when Murch states that "a good ten days of material was never filmed—Francis and the production team just ran out of time and money to shoot the entire script..."

What? Coppola walked away and never even shot 15 pages!? Really?

The funding for *The Godfather Pt. 2* was a big part of the reason for Coppola shutting down production on *The Conversation* two weeks early. This financial decision could have been disastrous, but it became a creative opportunity in the editing room.

Coppola entrusted Murch to make a film with the footage they had in hand. The story information on the missing 15 pages would have to be dodged in whatever way worked best.

I re-watched *The Conversation* with different eyes.

It is an editing masterpiece.

FILMS TO KNOW

Spoiler Alert: You're going to be watching films in film school. You're also going to be studying them.

You have to be more than just a passive viewer wanting to be entertained: you need to become an active viewer. You need to elevate your awareness of the complete craft of filmmaking, knowing *what* to look for, and *how* to look for it.

Filmmakers take characters and dialogue and bring them to life in the world of cinema. The masters of film are like great magicians: they make the magic look easy. As an active viewer, you have to watch and listen very closely to understand how they are creating their acts of illusion. When you set out to study how the magic of a film is created, you discover a complex construction made with many different parts.

Films are like finished jigsaw puzzle pictures: close scrutiny reveals the intricate pieces and shows you how it all fits together.

Knowing a film and truly understanding it requires you to break it down into its parts to examine how it's made. First, you have to see the whole thing to understand the world and fate of the characters. The construction of a film—how it's shaped and the way it's told—is going to be easier to grasp after you've seen it once and know the events of the story.

Watching films a second time helps you build your active viewer muscles. Repeat screenings and shot by shot analysis develops your sensibilities as a filmmaker: this is how you build creative muscles.

The goal of studying films is not to turn you into a trivia expert or movie critic. Filmmakers watch films for different reasons than regular audiences, but the sensations created by the story are always at the heart of the filmgoer's experience.

When you get caught up in the emotions of a character at any given point in a good film there can be so many things happening that it becomes impossible to separate it into parts, let alone figure out how all the parts are working together.

After you walk out of a theatre, you might recall a cool shot, an interesting location or an amazing action scene. But have you ever had zero recollection of the music?

Music is the universal language. It stirs up powerful emotions, and it can be a big part of the success of many films. How could anyone miss such an integral and important component? It happens all the time. When you study a film, you have to watch *and* listen.

Directors work with composers to bring music to the film and support the story. It's not wrong if the music seems to disappear and go unnoticed in some places. In many cases, this is the desired effect. We want audiences to enter into the world of the characters and forget they are watching a movie.

Film composers, like sound designers, weave their artistry into the fabric of the film. The irony is that a viewer may be completely engaged in a scene *because* of the sound and music. It's there and it's working on them, and they don't even realize it.

Film, like every profession, requires constant professional development. For a relatively young art form, there is a huge inventory of exceptional work to discover. To be a successful industry newcomer you have to keep current *and* you also need to know what's been done in the history of global cinema.

Stanley Kubrick is often cited as being an influence for many filmmakers. Kubrick was an avid moviegoer, but if the opening ten minutes left him cold, he was out. Kubrick was influenced by the original greats: Eisenstein, Griffith and Stroheim. He admired David Lean, Chaplin, Fellini, Bergman and Kazan. You can find lists of Kubrick's favourite films online.

Check out other filmmakers for their influences. Orson Welles claimed to have watched *Stagecoach* more than 40 times before he shot *Citizen Kane*. What was he looking for? How did watching *Stagecoach* influence him as a first-time film director? If you've seen *Stagecoach* you know it's nothing like *Citizen Kane*. But watching both films for camera height, camera angle, set design, lighting, composition, etc. is a film education in itself.

Jump into the world of cinema. Do your research, and design a screening schedule. You can do this at no cost by choosing a selection of films that are available in the library.

After you see a film that resonates with you, take the time to go the extra distance to learn a bit more about it. If you like the look of a film, take note of the cinematographer and production designer. Watch other projects they have done together. If you're impressed with an action scene, check out other films that the editor has worked on.

CREATIVE BINDER
YOUR TOP FILMS LIST

- **Select** some criteria. For example, study films that won Oscars for a specialization that you're interested in or the top prizewinners from Cannes;

- **Review** the list of the top 100 films. Films are ranked annually. You'll find *Vertigo, Citizen Kane, Chinatown, Sunset Boulevard* and *Rashomon* on most lists. Have you seen these classics?

- **Choose** a filmmaker. Watch their first film;

- **Listen** to a director commentary;

- **Screen** a documentary on a filmmaker or the 'making of' a film. For example, *Burden of Dreams,* or *Lost in La Mancha;*

- **Explore** genres: Thriller, Horror, Comedy, etc. Watch an early classic of a specific genre and compare it to a current release;
- **Create** your own 'top films list' and keep adding to it.

· ·

CREATIVE BINDER
FILM STUDIES

- **Choose** a film that you've heard is noteworthy but haven't seen. Watch it straight through;

- **Write** down your initial impressions on the themes, story, characters, images and dialogue. Who did you root for? What stayed with you?

- **Screen** it a second time putting greater focus on the specializations you're interested in: lighting, editing, camera movement, production design, etc. Stop and start. Freeze it. Rewind;

- **Select** a scene and turn off the sound. Break it into bits and pieces: shots, framing, angles, transitions, etc. Start it again but close your eyes and listen to the music, sound and dialogue;

- **Research** the film, read reviews, etc. This can lead you down many different rabbit holes where you can make surprising discoveries;

- **Read** your initial impressions again;
- **Write** your final thoughts about the scenes that drew you in, the emotions you felt. Note some of the cinematic elements used by the filmmaker to craft those moments.

• •

BEST DEAL IN TOWN

Years ago, I bought an all-access pass for the local film festival. It was a hefty cost at the time (even with the student discount) but it included the opening, closing and gala screenings with invited filmmakers in attendance.

My goal was to get as much value as possible out of this pass.

Some days I'd see as many as four films. I discovered fabulous worlds just by taking a chance on a title or an intriguing synopsis. I went to matinees, Q+A's and premieres. I covered my program with scribble notes.

After the closing gala, I did the math. Dollar for dollar it was an incredible deal. I had gone to the best theatres in town, enjoyed lots of new films and paid less than three dollars per show.

The expensive part was the popcorn.

Note to self: do that again.

INT. UNIVERSITY CLASSROOM - DAY

First day of film school. Twenty keen students sit quietly. The professor enters and
scrutinizes them from the lectern.

                    PROFESSOR
     Who is interested in cinematography?

More than half the class raise their hands.

                    PROFESSOR
     Who is interested in post-production?

Nine hands go up.

                    PROFESSOR
               How about producing?

Six hands.

                    PROFESSOR
                Production design?

Four.

                    PROFESSOR
               Who wants to direct?

Twenty hands reach up eagerly.

A few chuckles.

                    PROFESSOR
          So, who's been on a film set?

Heads turn. Eyes dart.

No hands go up.

EXPERIENCE

Previous production experience is not essential for film school but I strongly recommend it. Spending a day on a film set will open your eyes to the world of filmmaking.

Being an extra, a volunteer or observing on a film shoot or music video can give you valuable insight into how a set runs: the different jobs, set protocol, crew hierarchy.

How do you find opportunities?

- Bulletin boards at film schools are a place to start. You might see postings for background performers or assistant production roles, no experience necessary;
- Film clubs or television stations may need volunteers. Call them! Work a day for free;
- Check Craigslist under 'gigs' for creative, crew or talent listings;
- Create opportunities by getting involved with the community. Make phone calls, send emails, ask around.

Well before I directed my first feature, I set out to get experience in every creative role, mostly by working on student films. I learned by trial and error while putting in hundreds of hours. I gained a first-hand understanding of the demands and requirements of every position. I also met people who said they'd be willing to help me with my film. It's nice to be paid for a day's work, but there are different ways to find value in your efforts as you gain experience.

Watching a film crew and learning how a production works over the course of a day can help you develop your own ideas about how to manage a set and treat the people who will be working on your film.

Practical production experience matters. It's not required, but it says a lot if you can raise your hand when someone asks, "Who's been on a film set?"

TEAMWORK

Making a film involves a chain of people with different talents and abilities all working for a common goal. Teamwork requires a skillset *and* a mindset. Understanding your position and knowing how to work as part of a creative team is a requirement for the industry. Any experience you can gain in face-to-face, team-oriented activities is going to be a plus.

When you collaborate—or co-create—you align with people who share the same vision. Everyone pulls together in the interests of achieving the best outcome. In addition to responsibility, accountability, and structure, the success of any team relies on cooperation and communication.

Working on student films means working in small groups where everyone plays a role in helping to build each frame. A smooth-running show needs all crew positions to be filled. There's a hierarchy for a reason: people need to be responsible for their work and be graded on it.

Taking on a key creative role means you have to have opinions, make decisions, and have the perseverance to see your efforts through to completion. Having a point of view, giving feedback and evaluating feedback are vital parts of the filmmaking event. Just hitting the 'like' button may be fine for Facebook, but it won't take you very far in the industry. You need to know *what* you like and *why* you like it.

Working with people who aren't pulling their weight can be frustrating. In the film industry, people who show up late, fall asleep or don't do their jobs are likely to be fired—but it's not that way in most film programs. Figuring out what actions you or your team can take to deal with challenging personnel situations are learning opportunities: unexpected things are going to happen.

Relationships are one of the most important features of film school. Make the effort to meet people in the program who are outside of your class. Value every connection you make. Even if it's not a comfortable fit at first, remember that people grow, skills develop and situations change. You don't know it yet, but these may be the people who hire you in the future, or maybe you'll hire them.

MANAGING CREATIVE TEAMS

Student filmmaking teams may present unique challenges because you are not always in control of who you are partnered with. In the industry, particularly television, this is quite common.

A difficult team experience in film school can be an excellent opportunity to learn. If anything, you can find out how to recover, accept and move on from disappointment without it affecting your career.

Leading creative teams requires clearly stated goals and a collaborative approach. Great things can happen when teams are inspired and motivated by strong, effective leadership.

Some suggestions for creative team leaders:

- Be a coach, not a commandant;

- Build trust. Set the example;

- Clarify the challenge, task or problem. Seek agreement;

- Ask simple, open questions. Listen to the answers;

- Solicit possible solutions, ideas or strategies. Gather as many as possible. Filter accordingly;

- Set realistic goals, expectations and timelines;

- Be discreet when calling attention to mistakes made by members of the team. Pull people aside, or speak in private;

- Be kind. Thank others for their efforts, talent and contribution;

- Remember to ABC: Always Be Co-creating;

- Aim for the WIN-WIN-WIN result. That's where you win, they win, and the show wins!

FEEDBACK SANDWICH

Filmmakers want feedback on works in progress. Once a film is finished, it's too late for suggestions because they can't go back and make changes.

How do you give constructive feedback? Try the feedback sandwich: start with the positive, end with the positive, and put some of the critical stuff in the middle.

To be respectful of the opportunity, you have to be engaged as an active viewer with the intention of giving a detailed response. You want to have the best possible viewing conditions with no distractions. You should take good notes and organize them before sharing.

- **Start** your feedback with the good points: what you liked, what was good and what's working.

- **Move on** to what didn't work. Note where you were confused, bored, or ahead of the story and felt that you knew what was going to happen next. Point out a moment, a performance or a line of dialogue that didn't feel genuine or authentic. Be specific, your comments may lead to something that can be adjusted and finessed.

- **Close** with positive comments. Build on the good things. Make a suggestion or two that you feel might improve the work and see how it's received by the filmmakers.

Sound and music are usually unfinished when you screen works in progress. Frame your comments to consider the value they will bring.

Rough-cut screenings are a critical stage in the fine-tuning process of completing a film. Your fellow filmmakers will appreciate sincere and thoughtful feedback.

You will, too.

THANK YOU FOR SHARING

Film is a collective experience. It's important and helpful for filmmakers to show their work in progress and get reactions from an audience. A rough-cut screening with a robust critique lets a creative team gauge how their story is working, and what adjustments could be made in order to improve it.

I was invited to join an advanced production class to review their unfinished final projects. They were uncomfortably quiet when it came to offering feedback, good or bad. It's not that they didn't have opinions, they were just reluctant to speak up. I pressed them to find out why.

"We have to keep working together. I don't want to say it's bad or say what I think," said one student.

Yikes! That's not the way to go. You need to engage even if you don't particularly like the work. The filmmakers are not obliged to make changes based on your critique.

I asked everyone to **SHARE** their thoughts. They quickly found their voices using this easy to remember acronym:

S   Support - what did you like?

H   Be Honest - your opinion matters, but be kind;

A   Acknowledge what worked – there's always something;

R   Recommendations - limit to two or three;

E   Encourage – build the relationship.

Example:

There were some good moments and the performances are working. The opening was strong but the last half needs more attention, mostly with the dialogue. I felt I was ahead of the story and knew what was coming.

You do a good job of building the stakes. The tension really ramps up in the final argument. Maybe try and trim the dialogue or get out of that second scene in the hallway a little earlier. Just a thought.

If you make some changes and you'd like me to take another look, I'm in.

PITCHING

Q: What is pitching?

A: It's an exercise in persuasion.

Pitching is the term used for presenting your project, your story or your ideas in a convincing manner to someone whose interests and approval you are seeking.

You probably have more experience with this than you realize. Think about times when you've tried to get someone to go along with you, to get them excited about your choices or suggestions. Think about how you have swayed decisions with your friends and family: getting them to say 'yes' by selling them on the benefits and convincing them that your idea is a good one.

People pitch their story ideas in the film industry and in film school. It's not always the best ideas that get picked, sometimes it's the best pitch.

Sooner or later, you'll have to find and train your inner salesman in order to make your projects happen. You're going to need people to support and believe in your ideas in order to get your films produced. This is why you pitch.

What makes a good pitch? The idea, the content and the presentation.

Let's start with the presentation. Pitching can happen anywhere, anytime. When someone shows interest in a story or a film you want to make—that is a chance for you to pitch. You might have one minute; you might have ten. You may be talking with one person, or a boardroom full of suits. Having a handful of different approaches for different situations is always a good plan.

The pitching presentation is a combination of sales techniques, marketing ideas and public speaking. Rehearsal makes a difference. Your pitch needs to be sincere and heartfelt, but it shouldn't feel memorized. It needs to be exciting and fresh, and that comes from your enthusiasm and your performance.

Let's look at the content. If you only have one minute to present something, you have to make a decision on which aspects you're going to pitch. You can't tell the whole story, nor does anyone want to hear it. So how are you going to pitch your great film in 60 seconds?

There are three parts that build out the content of a pitch. First, you need a strong opener: something gripping, something unique that engages your listener and hooks them in the first 15 seconds. It could be the theme, the character, the situation or the major dramatic question. You want to fire up your audience's imagination, especially in a one-on-one situation. You have to get them interested off the top and then you have to keep them listening.

The second part, or middle section, can be tricky. You only have about 30 seconds for your talking points here. Keep it short and snappy as you expand on details or add elements. Whatever you do, don't overstay your welcome.

A strong close is the hallmark of a good pitch. It can be a statement, a dilemma or anything that builds the drama and conflict. It can even be a question, but it's important to leave your audience with a satisfying and thought-provoking conclusion. Fifteen seconds here and you have reached the one-minute time limit.

Learn how to pitch a short film. Have fun with it. Practice it. Pitch what you think is compelling and let your audience know why this film has to be made.

Is it a timely topic? Is there a big question? Is there a fabulous villain?

You can practice pitching anytime someone asks you what you're working on. If you're at a party and you speak with five different people, you have a chance to try five different approaches.

Keep it brief; keep it interesting, and; watch your listener closely to gauge their reaction. After every pitch, take time to mentally summarize what worked, what needs adjustment and what other things you might try next time around.

Pitches evolve. A poor pitch makes your next one better because you learned what didn't work. That's why people practice and try different versions.

In school and the industry, you will be pitching. Why not start now? All you need is an idea for a story, a character, a genre, a title—and someone to ask, "What are you working on?"

CREATIVE BINDER
LEARN TO PITCH

I've encountered some interesting pitching techniques on used car lots. Talking with a good salesperson is a lesson in the language of persuasion: they are constantly pitching.

Even if I wasn't in the market for a particular model, I loved watching them work. Obviously, they have to get people excited about buying a car, or else they won't be selling many.

One rainy day, I pointed out a two-inch puddle in the trunk of a '68 Mustang. The pivot was classic and he didn't miss a beat: "Yeah, Yeah. It leaks a bit, but look at the upholstery!"

You can have fun learning how to pitch, but be careful on used car lots or you might drive away with a clunker.

There are safer ways to learn:

Search crowdfunding sites where filmmakers are trying to raise money. You'll find lots of pitch videos. Study the ones that you think are effective. Study the ones you don't like, too. Think about why they didn't work for you.

Research film pitch tutorials online. You'll find plenty of examples.

Screen *The Player,* directed by Robert Altman. Watch it the first time for the great film that it is. Watch it again for the different pitching events: where they happen, how they work, why they work—or why they don't.

. . . .

PUBLIC SPEAKING

How does it feel when all eyes in the room are on you?

Whether it's in front of a big audience or at a small gathering, most people are terrified of being in the spotlight: speaking in public is the number one fear for a major percentage of the population.

Stage fright happens. Some people panic; some freeze; some faint. In order to lead a team or a creative project, you must cultivate the confidence to present yourself and your ideas in a group setting.

Addressing an audience and being comfortable (or at least *looking* comfortable) is not easy for most people. Rehearsal and practice can make you feel more prepared, but walking on stage will always get the heart pounding.

Developing your public speaking skills through study and practice, on your own, has an inherent design flaw: it's all dress rehearsal. Standing up and presenting to a real audience, and experiencing the pressure of the authentic event is something that a lot of people don't get an opportunity to do.

You can improve your presentations by emulating the pacing, delivery and strategies of memorable speakers. Learning how to engage an audience, control nervousness and keep your train of thought are talents that will help you in film school.

Your delivery determines and shapes your connection with the audience. Relaxation and breathing techniques are helpful. Having an awareness of your voice tone and body language is important. But finding that personal style that conveys your unique qualities is vital: your passion, your sense of humour and your confidence are your greatest assets.

The content of your presentation needs careful attention. It needs to be organized, planned and rehearsed to help ensure that everything goes smoothly.

In order to keep and sustain your audience's attention, you need to watch and gauge their involvement. You know what it's like when you're talking with someone who's distracted or avoiding eye contact: it's uncomfortable. If your audience is actively listening, you'll be able to tell. If they're not, you'll need to adjust.

Using projected slides for presentations requires preparation. Visual aids can be helpful, but too much information or too much text on a screen can be overwhelming. The audience is there to listen to you. Use slides and visuals to support your presentation, not dominate it.

The ability to communicate in a way that motivates people has tremendous value. If you direct, you'll be talking with actors; if you're the head of a department, you'll be talking with crew; if you produce, you'll be meeting with financiers.

You want others to see you as genuine, consistent and personable to work with. Self-observation is difficult and tracking how you come across in any situation is even harder.

It might help to practice your presentation on video. Look to keep it upbeat, and natural: kind of like you're thinking on your feet and having fun with something that you're passionate about. Use language that makes people comfortable. There's no value in challenging your audience with obscure terms or big words. You want to get them on your side. Be animated. Use physical gestures that loosen you up or help you to emphasize your main points.

Presentations, like good stories, need a beginning, middle and end. A memorable speaker pulls the audience in with a strong setup; keeps building through the middle; and closes with a brilliant finish—like a gold medal gymnastic routine.

BEST TIP IN THE BOOK

If you want to be a filmmaker, take an acting class.

Find a group that's appropriate for your age and experience level. There are classes for newcomers with no prior experience.

Of course, there will be nerves. And there will also be fun. It's important to find the fun in a beginner's class. Look for the right energy and a sense of play.

Understanding the actor experience through your own filter will help you going forward as a filmmaker. The sensation of being open and vulnerable, of being a character that's not yourself, accessing new and different emotions—this is what actors do.

Scene study, memorizing lines, rehearsing the action—it's not as easy as it looks.

Try it. Embrace it. Act! React!!

People are going to watch you.

You are going to watch other people.

SPOILER ALERT: This is what happens in film school.

SKILLS

Basic knowledge of digital video editing and a grasp of how to manage media on a timeline can alleviate a lot of stress and frustration when it comes to making your first student film. Free trials of editing software, like Avid or Adobe Premiere, are available. You can also watch the basics in action with free tutorials on Youtube or sign up for Lynda. com. Technical skills have value, however, social skills and life skills are going to be equally, if not more, important. In today's competitive world, the ability to get along with others is essential.

This is the communication industry: people skills are required. Being a filmmaker means you are part of a creative team. Teams want mediators, problem-solvers and critical thinkers. You need to know how to interact with other creative people. How you communicate matters.

Film teams share information. Communicating ideas and details accurately relies on everyone in the chain. A miscommunication caused by a typo, an omission or a simple misunderstanding are things you definitely try to avoid.

When in doubt, follow the 21st century film student best practices: treat others as you would like to be treated. Be an engaged listener, a good speaker and an impeccable writer.

Nonverbal communication—body language—is also something to focus on. How you look and act sends a strong message long before you open your mouth. Your spoken message may be positive, but your expression and eyes may be saying something contrary; posture and distraction may give others the impression that you'd rather be somewhere else.

If you feel that you can improve your social and communication skills—start now. Changing a habit can be challenging. You have some wiggle room for error in film school, but the industry will be less forgiving.

STORYTELLING

From cave paintings to summer blockbusters, stories explain how the world works and how we fit into it. We learn from stories. We're programmed to process them.

The history of the world is the history of storytelling. Through stories, we come to understand social rules and behaviour; cultural norms and aberrations; other people's emotions and reactions.

Stories help us survive.

People from all cultures consume stories from an early age. There's a natural inclination to believe that anyone can tell a story and for the most part that's true, but telling a *good* story takes talent and skill.

As a storyteller, you must know the world of your characters. You have to lead your audience through the details of the story by telling them what they need to know and when they need to know it.

As a visual storyteller, the settings, situations and performances need to fuse and create a wholly compelling tale: this is the benchmark for the successful filmmaker. The images and sounds are important but the heart of a film is in the story and characters.

Story is what suffers most in the majority of student films. You need to craft an original story before you can make an original film. Stories are about people with desires and struggles. If you feel that you're lacking experiences or story material to draw on, make a decision to change that: meet new people, explore different neighbourhoods, attend unique events.

People want stories that capture the spirit, energy and imagination of a generation, a country or a culture. The filmmakers of tomorrow need to craft brave new narratives told from their unique vantage points.

The audience knows what they like: a satisfying story with interesting characters in a world that they are willing to believe. We have all grown up as members of the audience. In film school, you are the storyteller.

BONUS TIP: The experience of making a film is better if you have a personal connection with the material. Find stories and characters that are of particular interest to you.

CREATIVE BINDER
PECHAKUCHA

In 2006, there was a special evening of exclusive presentations at the Cannes Film Festival—but they weren't films, they were PechaKucha.

PechaKucha is a timed slideshow with a simple formula:

- 20 slides
- 20 seconds each
- Spoken word narration

PechaKucha is a lot like filmmaking: you select your topic, write your script and create a series of accompanying images.

The slides are set to auto-advance to keep the overall timing of the presentation fixed. This visual format builds the presentation framework for the speaker and keeps presentations concise, dynamic and energized.

Research Pecha Kucha presentations online.

Generate concepts that work for the format.

Choose one and build an outline.

Create the slides.

Write the narration for the timed slides.

Practice and record your presentation to evaluate it for yourself.

When you're ready for an audience—go for it! Organize your own PechaKucha event, just like they do at Cannes.

. . . .

PHOTOGRAPHY

For over a century, every frame of film was a mechanically produced image of art captured by a camera and developed through a photochemical process. The equipment was cumbersome, expensive and finicky. There were lots of moving parts and an ever-present risk of failure. This has changed.

Digital technology has made every stage of the filmmaking event easier, safer and cheaper—but making a *good* film is still hard.

Thinking in pictures is central to the filmmaker's craft. The first films were silent and told stories with only images. Pioneering directors used written text in frames to explain specific story points. The advent of sound allowed dialogue and narration to take the place of text, but the challenge for filmmakers has always been to use the language of cinema to convey the story through imagery.

The time you spend familiarizing yourself with the techniques of photography will pay off when you get to film school. Understanding lenses—how they work and why different ones are used—is what you'll be learning in cinematography class. Don't wait until you're in school to explore the work of photographers and cinematographers.

Try different looks, techniques and approaches:

- Focus
- Depth
- Shadows
- Composition

Practising, experimenting and manipulating your own images with filters, contrast and colour correction is something you can do on a smartphone. You select, control and organize the content of the frame. What makes a good photo? Study the work of great photographers for techniques and approaches that you like. It's not about copying someone else's photography; it's about understanding the fundamentals and applying them to your own work.

You can't begin to talk about photography without talking about light. Cinematographers tell stories with light. Whether you are inside or outside, the lighting makes the shot: no light, no image.

What makes a frame 'work' depends on many factors. You may have taken thousands of pictures but studying and analyzing photos—particularly ones with intentional lighting—will help you create stronger narrative images: images with meaning.

Different lenses create different moods. Telephoto lenses compress space and flatten an image; wide-angle lenses expand space and create greater depth. The best lens to use for an image depends on the story you want to tell.

Some film schools ask for a photography sample in your application materials. Juries are looking to see if you can capture a feeling, convey an emotion and tell a story in a frame. A notable style or purely aesthetic appeal can also make your work stand out.

Dynamic imagery helps tell a dramatic story.

CREATIVE BINDER
24 FRAMES

A top-ranked program in Europe asks potential students for a set of photographs on three subjects: landscape, portrait, and reporter's observation of an event. Your choice of content and composition, along with your overall technique and presentation of 24 frames can be the tipping point that gets you invited to an interview.

Try this exercise:

Gather your photos. Do you need to take new ones or do you have a selection to choose from? Should they be black and white or colour? Is there a theme, a concept or some way that the photos work as a grouping?

Choose 10 or 12 photos on each of the three above-mentioned subjects.

Present them to a few trusted sources. Which ones are their favourites? Why? Ask questions, take notes. Is there a feeling or emotion captured in the frame? How are they interpreting and evaluating it?

Organize the feedback and track the favourites.

Select the photos that were consistently popular and create your top 24 (eight frames on each subject.)

Analyze them for similar features: tone, content, style, composition, theme, etc.

New Deal: repeat this exercise with completely different images. Get feedback from new sources. Find fresh eyes, people who haven't seen any of your other photos.

This is good practice for learning to evaluate feedback and assess criticism, and the stakes are relatively low. It also helps build your portfolio assets.

. . . .

DRAWING

It's time to embrace the essential tools of creativity: pen and paper. They are fundamental in filmmaking. Keep them close by.

Making a film is an exercise in finding, revising and improving ideas: tracking changes on scripts, jotting down details of a discussion or a hastily written note on a napkin to remember the great idea you just had. These basic tools are indispensable.

The methods for developing visual ideas are different for everyone. Regardless of the approach, the goal is the same: getting your thoughts into a physical form so that you can review, evaluate and share them with others. I recommend pen and paper because plug-in technology and digital files are not always practical in the challenging environments of filmmaking. Furthermore, the best-laid plans can change fast on set. It's good to have tools that will work under any circumstances.

Pen and paper help your ideas evolve and expand. You don't have to be a great artist, just get your hand moving across the page. You'll be glad you did.

SKETCHING

Sketching is expressive. It should be fun and enjoyable. It's not about what's right or wrong: it's about generating ideas for the work in progress.

A sketch is fast and immediate. It can be as simple as a few lines: a quick test to see if your idea has merit—especially a visual idea.

A sketch can clarify a shot you're planning by showing the rudimentary arrangement of elements in the frame. It enables your fellow filmmakers to better understand your ideas and helps them work more effectively with you.

Sketching frees you up creatively. It's not supposed to be perfect. It's a process of thinking visually. You don't have to be fancy, you just need to get your ideas across. You can save many hours and words by showing a simple drawing for the composition of a shot.

Sketches are easy to change or revise. You can draw over them or you can throw them out and start anew. A rough sketch of a frame is also called a 'thumbnail' and it should take less than 10 seconds to do. Thumbnails can save the day if you want to quickly rework an idea on set.

Sketches can become more detailed when you have a clear idea about how you want to see specific moments of your film. They might start as static frames and then evolve by linking together to form the building blocks of an elegant camera move. Making the effort to sketch out your ideas helps you develop the visual concepts for bringing your film to life.

STORYBOARDING

Storyboards are drawings of the shots that are needed to tell the story set inside a frame. Steven Spielberg creates thousands of storyboards when he prepares to direct a film. He throws hundreds away and then creates many, many more. It's all part of his process to make his directing vision stronger and clearer in pre-production.

Storyboards have been used for a long time to help different departments communicate and coordinate in getting a film made. It's common to see pages of storyboards for the day's work posted in the camera truck or production office so that everyone knows what the crew is planning to shoot.

A skilled storyboard artist finesses the director's visual ideas. Professional storyboards incorporate perspective, camera height, camera angle and even the suggested lens. They can indicate movement by the camera or a character by using directional arrows, either in the images or outside the frames.

Most directors like to work with a storyboard artist for stunts, action scenes or visual effect sequences. Storyboarding the shots, frame-by-frame, facilitates production, scheduling and budgeting.

Storyboarding is pre-visualizing. 'Pre-viz', as it's called, is popular in effects-driven productions, even to the point of creating animated storyboards or 'animatics' to show the flow of images and get a sense for the pacing of a scene.

Producers are responsible for managing the time and money in filmmaking. Directors who share their vision can garner the support they need to realize their best work. Storyboards make it easier for producers to understand and champion the director's plan. With enough lead-time, every department can have input and make their best contribution to the principle photography.

There are directors who don't use storyboards. Some prefer to improvise: responding to the actors' choices, solving problems and finding opportunities as part of the creative evolution of a shot. But student directors who are making their first films can benefit from planning all of the shots they need to tell their story. It doesn't have to be written in stone. Changing or reworking shots are part of the learning curve for all filmmakers.

Building your scenes on paper will always serve you well. Find instructional videos to help you develop the basic skills. Like most things, the more you do it—the better you get.

CREATIVE BINDER
STORYBOARDS

Buy a sketchpad, some pencils and a sharpener. You're going to draw, create and have fun. Fine Art is not the goal.

Watch sketching tutorial videos to review the basics and beginner tips. Many are available. Practice, loosen up and improve your sketching skills.

Watch storyboard tutorials. Look for techniques on perspective, depth and how arrows can help explain movement in a drawing.

Think how you would visually portray the nursery rhyme:

Humpty Dumpty sat on a wall.
Humpty Dumpty had a great fall.
All the King's horses and all the King's men
Couldn't put Humpty together again.

List the shots and dynamic frames that you'll need, like a low angle shot looking up at Humpty, and a high angle shot looking down.

Sketch with simple lines and geometric shapes. Vary the image size. Exaggerate the height of the wall. Have the wall cross diagonally through the frame. Sketch a frame of Humpty in a wide shot. Sketch a close-up. Don't worry about facial expression.

Draw an arrow to suggest Humpty falling off the wall. In another frame, draw an arrow to suggest Humpty's fall into the shot and the messy landing.

Sketch a frame that looks over the shoulders of the King's men looking at broken Humpty.

Storyboards are frames that visually tell the story. For our purposes, keep the detail limited. It's more important to think about composition, foreground and background.

Have fun! Draw different versions.

Fill your sketchpad.

. . . .

DRAFTING

Drafting is the term for technical drawing and it's critical for plans and proposals where precision is important. Filmmakers need technical drawings for floor plans, design illustrations, set construction, special prop construction, etc.

Drafting involves different perspectives: front, side and overhead. The overhead or 'bird's eye view' of a set or interior location gives the dimensions and details of the floor plan; an essential planning document for directors, production designers and camera teams.

Floor plans help with furniture placement, character movement and lighting concepts. Simple notations can quickly explain the layout, windows, doorways and flow of action. Once you know how the action is going to play, you can figure out where you might put the camera.

Creating precision documents can be realized and modified quickly using design and drafting software. There are different options for different requirements, and in some cases, fully-free versions are available for students. However, a ruler, tape measure, and graph paper can be all that an independent filmmaker needs for coming up with usable hand-drawn floor plans.

PART IV

Every idea you have has potential, but not all will

be suitable to make the transformation into film.

*Ideas are like rabbits. You get a couple
and learn how to handle them, and
pretty soon you have a dozen.*

— JOHN STEINBECK

*A work of art is the trace of
a magnificent struggle.*

— ROBERT HENRI, THE ART SPIRIT

*My film school would allow you to experience
a certain climate of excitement of the mind,
and would produce people with spirit,
a furious inner excitement, and a burning
flame within. This is what ultimately creates
films. Technical knowledge inevitably
becomes dated; the ability to adapt to
change will always be more important.*

— WERNER HERZOG

CREATIVE ASSETS

Welcome to the most important section of this book. Film students need to have original creative assets in hand well before day one.

Good stories are key to your outcomes. Schools don't hand out original ideas, you must have your own for the films that you want to make. These ideas have to be realistic for production at the student level. An understanding of the limitations in low-budget filmmaking is helpful when you're developing your creative inventory. These limitations are common sense, for the most part. For example, a scene in a grand ballroom filled with distinguished people in tuxedos and evening gowns is beyond the scope of student productions.

Ideas are your raw materials: ideas become films. How that transformation happens is kind of like the caterpillar and the butterfly: they are the same entity, but the caterpillar goes through a metamorphosis as it changes into its new form. You will be far further ahead if you have a clear understanding of the stages that are necessary to transform your ideas into film.

IDEAS

Ideas? Yes, please! I hope you've got a bunch of them. More is definitely better.

Ideas are like reels of unexposed film. They are latent images on an imaginary projector that's running in your head. These undeveloped images need to be processed or they'll simply remain as thoughts. Ideas that you fail to act on leave you with nothing in hand.

Ideas can come from anywhere but you also need strategies to generate them. Waiting for the muse and faithfully believing that great ideas will surely come is not the best plan when you have scripts to write and deadlines to meet.

Making films requires a lot of energy. If you shoot a script that doesn't work at the story level, it's not likely to be a satisfying filmmaking experience. I believe in experimentation and taking calculated risks, but the filmmaker who starts with a solid story will have a better chance of making a film they can be proud of.

Most ideas don't arrive in a fully-realized form as feasible stories that you can just run out and film. They start off as fragments: random moments, overheard whispers, awkward situations.

Story ideas are everywhere. Sometimes they grow from an image, an observation or a line from a poem. Any of these can be a jumping off point for your imagination.

Ideas need to be captured. They need to be grabbed from thin air and secured into words, drawings, or plans. Once you have an idea on the page it can be assessed.

Write down memorable moments that you have experienced directly: the times you laughed, cried or were frightened. Keep searching for memories that are notable and entertaining, ones you can tell a story about.

Recollect situations that surprised you with the way they turned out.

Recall stories that you've heard other people tell.

Eavesdrop if the opportunity presents itself.

Remember your dreams. Keep track of them. Your dream world is a fertile ground for idea generation. They may be confusing, abstract and incomplete—with no beginning, middle or end—but they might hold a clue or piece to another puzzle. Many people keep journals or diaries of their dreams.

Write about people you know. (Don't worry, they'll never recognize themselves.)

Your experiences are important. So are your imaginings. Random thoughts can develop into stories or contribute to other ones that you're working on—start collecting them.

An idea may start out quite grandiose and eventually be refined into something that can be completed with the resources on hand. Don't censor yourself, but it might be wise to hold back on your big ideas until you see how you do with the smaller ones.

You're going to need ideas for stories. Every idea has potential but not all will be suitable to make the transformation into film. To show up at film school without ideas, stories and scripts that are feasible for production at the student level is to arrive unprepared.

CREATIVE BINDER
STORY IDEA GENERATOR

Write a short description of:

- **A defining moment**—something pivotal that shaped your behaviour or another person's behaviour;

- **An emotional event**—joy, sorrow, regret, betrayal, fear, dread, resentment, friendship, love, devotion;

- **A learning situation**—an epiphany, a breakthrough, a lesson, an encounter with someone in a position of power;

- **A surprising situation**—when someone made you feel important, angry, stupid, smart or afraid;

- **A special achievement**;

- **A shared moment**—between friends or strangers;

- **A secret** you just had to tell somebody;
- **An incident** you observed happening to someone else;
- **Begin with**: This is a story about…

Write two or three paragraphs.

Embrace the Five W's: Who, What, When, Where, and Why.

Try to generate a new story idea every day. If you come up with more, that's even better. The goal of the exercise is to generate A LOT OF IDEAS! Once you have ideas to choose from, you can select the best ones. Quantity leads to quality.

• •

SCENE OUTLINES

Creative writing courses for production students are most effective when they are linked to learning and practising the construction of scenes. Starting out with a collection of good ideas and having them in hand ahead of time is a must.

Scenes have dramatic structure. They are compact stories, or at least they should be. A good scene has a point of view—and a beginning, middle, and end.

The goal of a scene is to make your audience feel something. A well-written scene explores a situation where the emotional state of a character changes. For example, if a character starts out happy about something, the end of the scene should contrast or counter that feeling. If nothing changes, you may not have a scene.

Scenes need conflict, challenges, opposing forces, tough decisions. No conflict, no story. Characters make interesting choices when they're under pressure. The stakes are up to you, but something has to happen that changes the world of a character, possibly forever.

Scenes emerge from character, place and action. As the storyteller, you choose and design these elements. You invent them or exaggerate them. Developing and shaping the drama, comedy or tension is your responsibility as the screenwriter.

Award-winning shorts have a powerful turning point, a curve-ball that changes and alters the outcome. A good story twist is one that the audience didn't see coming.

Writing and directing a scene with three or more characters is something to aspire to. For learning filmmakers, stay with the basics: two people, your age, in one location. This is something that you can realize at film school.

Make your scene about one idea: the simplest ideas can become the most entertaining films.

CREATIVE BINDER
SCENE OUTLINES

Select an idea from the previous Idea Generator exercise. Keep it to one location and two characters.

Write four paragraphs in the third person following this plan:

First paragraph: Describe the main character. Set up the world, introduce the dramatic situation and the secondary character.

Second paragraph: This is the first act of your story. Describe the incident, action or event that creates change. Set up the conflict here.

Third paragraph: Build the story. List the problems, difficulties or obstacles that need to be overcome and worked through by the main character. What does the character want?

Fourth paragraph: This is the third (and final) act where you describe the climax of the scene. How does the situation get resolved?

The story in this outline form should fit easily on one page. It doesn't have to be perfect.

This is the starting place for a scene that you could shoot in one day with a small crew.

• •

SCRIPTS

A well-written script is a great accomplishment. Scripts are the written plans for films. There's a template to be followed: an accepted industry standard known as 'master scene' format. Professional writers use licensed software, such as Final Draft, which automatically formats the different parts of a script, such as dialogue, character names and description. Popular and free alternatives are Amazon Storywriter and WriterDuet.

Writing in screenplay format helps the production process with planning, scheduling and budgeting. Though the style, content and manner of writing for the screen have changed over time, the template remains basically the same.

What's important for the beginning filmmaker is to learn how to write effectively in the accepted industry style. Well-known screenwriters sometimes defy the format and use unconventional strategies. Advancing the art of cinema may be your goal, but know the rules first.

A properly written screenplay is a primary building block in the filmmaking process. Risk-averse producers and film financiers prefer scripts in the familiar industry format. You need to show that you know how to write a screenplay. Once you know the rules, you can break them. If you have success, others will be more willing to take a chance and go along with something different or innovative.

Scripts don't require dialogue but you may need to demonstrate that you understand the function of dialogue if you're seeking consideration from a top-ranked school. Dialogue is more than conversation, it's an exchange of meaningful information that reveals something about the characters and their conflict. Well-written dialogue is the life-blood of great characters.

Dialogue should sound natural. It should provide the essential details that are necessary to advance the story. Too many words spoken by one character can feel like a speech when you put it on film.

Avoid the small talk (Hi! Hi! How are you? Good! It's really hot today. Yeah, it sure is. I hope it cools down. Yeah, me too.): your audience will thank you. Removing the niceties of a normal conversation while keeping the drama front and center is the hallmark of good dialogue and good screenwriting.

Make sure you know your characters: their background, strengths, fears and flaws. Every character needs to have their own individual voice. Their choice of words, the way they react, the flow of information and the stakes of the conflict work in concert to create memorable, believable and interesting characters.

Screenplay format is one of the most difficult forms. It's not prose; it's not a story to be printed and published; it's supposed to be something else—it's supposed to become a film.

CREATIVE BINDER
30-MINUTE
STORY DRILL

No more staring at the blank page on the computer screen. This helpful exercise gives you a structure for developing a story or an idea for a film script in one sitting. In just half an hour you'll be much further along by organizing your thoughts and mapping out how your story begins, builds and ends.

Set a timer.

Start Writing:

- 2 minutes — I want to make a film on… (list as many ideas as you can.)

- 2 minutes — The idea I like most is... (develop a story idea about it.)

- 2 minutes — I could include these moments... (list as many as possible and don't censor yourself.)

- 2 minutes — Expand on a moment or event.

- 2 minutes — Expand on another moment.

- 2 minutes — Articulate the dramatic conflict.

- 2 minutes — Create options for how to resolve it.

- 2 minutes — Describe the antagonist and what's at stake.

- 2 minutes — Rough out a scene that highlights the conflict.

- 2 minutes — Come up with an opening scene and an opening image.

- 2 minutes — Put your scenes in order and create a timeline.

- 2 minutes — The title of this story is... (list as many titles as you can.)

- 2 minutes — Compose a short synopsis with a beginning, middle and end: three or four sentences.

Use the remaining 4 minutes to expand your synopsis and add more details.

Put it all together and file it under your favourite title for this story.

• •

CREATIVE BINDER
SHORT SCRIPTS

Deadlines for creative assignments can be nerve-wracking for many people. Here's how to stay ahead:

Prepare story ideas and show up on day one with a handful of short, doable outlines or scripts. The struggle to write original scripts is considerably more challenging when you have the additional responsibilities of a full-time academic schedule.

Write with guidelines in mind. When it comes to content, schools have rules. Guidelines generally include: no weapons, no drugs, no driving scenes, no stunts, no nudity, no open flames, no tobacco, no sexually suggestive scenes, no gratuitous violence and cautions for profanity. Knowing the rules allows you to craft stories that fit inside your school's policies.

Page count is important for student projects—aim for five to seven pages if you have one or two days to shoot.

Locations should be kept to a minimum. Moving the team and packing up the gear takes up valuable time. Aim for one location per day.

If you want to graduate with films, arrive with scripts you can shoot.

Select a few of your favourite scene outlines and write them in screenplay format. The first draft is not going to sparkle like a diamond. Don't be shy. Start writing and get those first drafts out of the way.

. . . .

MAKING CONTACT

In my student days, while table-reading screenplays with fellow classmates in a creative writing workshop, a stranger appeared at the classroom door. He interrupted the teacher and introduced himself as a filmmaker from another school. He explained that he would be making a short film as a final project in his program, but he didn't have a script. He'd gone to several schools with writing courses and spoken with many students, but he was still searching for a good story. He wrote his number on the board, thanked everyone and left.

I was intrigued, but hesitant. I'd written a script in the previous term called *Making Contact*. It was a story with two characters based on an urban myth about a campus ghost. I gave it another read, waited for a week, then picked up the phone and asked if he was still looking for short screenplays.

"I most definitely am," he replied. "You're the only one who's called!"

Six months later I was invited to the premiere and saw my first writing credit on the big screen. The title had changed and so had the story: a dream sequence had been added, another scene was dropped and the ending was different. It was an eye-opening lesson into the collaborative process of filmmaking and how scripts get revised through the realities of production.

The moral of the story: filmmakers need original screenplays.

Start writing. What are you waiting for?

PORTFOLIO

If you plan on applying to top-ranked programs, your portfolio will be a vital part of the selection process. Schools set standards for their students when they require a portfolio. It raises the bar for the classmates whom you'll be partnered with and the benchmark for the education that you'll receive.

A strong portfolio demonstrates that you understand the overall filmmaking process and have the knowledge, confidence and expertise that it takes to make a film. Your portfolio offers examples of what you're capable of creating with the resources that you have. If you're up to date with the exercises in previous chapters, you're in good shape to start polishing these assets into support materials.

Organizing your creative assets into categories—visual materials, writing samples, personal statement—gives you a flexible resource base to draw on. You want to keep adding to this base: improving, revising but never deleting. This lets you customize and refine any submissions you make to other programs.

It's good to get feedback on your portfolio, but be careful who you listen to. Good intentions are all around. Your kind friends and family may be loving and supportive, but they won't be on the admissions committee. Fair, unbiased evaluation will help you step back and critically assess your work. Your portfolio is about you: it will succeed or fail on its own merits, so take charge of your submission. It's never wrong to trust your instincts.

Remember that every presentation is important. Hastily throwing something together is never a good plan. Committees can review hundreds of portfolios every year. The first cull is often separating out the ones that are complete, inspired and well presented. You definitely want to make this first cut.

Materials to be submitted need to meet the posted parameters. Providing your work in the correct format and size is a requirement. Be sure to comply with all due dates, limits and specifications.

I've served on advisory committees and interview panels for student admissions and the most important tip that I want to pass along is the concept of authorship. Whatever you submit, it should be written, directed or created by you. Your portfolio needs to shout, 'I MADE THIS!'

Avoid sharing creative credit. This may sound harsh, but it deserves serious consideration. Any submissions that are co-written or co-directed will be perceived as a merge of talents. A film that is co-authored makes it difficult for anyone to fairly and accurately evaluate the work of each individual. It's not the responsibility of the committee to decipher your contribution in a shared credit. They are not mind readers.

The admissions process is specific to each school. Those who don't get into the programs of their choice see it as a flawed system but there are standards that guide these committees. Most importantly: every applicant is to receive fair and equitable treatment. For that reason alone, some schools stipulate that they will not accept co-authored materials.

Top-ranked schools have comprehensive portfolio requirements. Portfolios can be heavily weighted in the assessment of short-list candidates for three main reasons:

>It validates experience and commitment;
>
>It demonstrates creative interests and abilities;
>
>It facilitates equitable review and consideration.

Portfolio submissions help schools filter out students who may not be suited for their kind of program or ready to take on the creative and academic workload at this point in time.

Schools want students whom they feel will excel in their program and become notable alumni.

Your portfolio is your best chance to make a strong first impression. Make it thoughtful; make it organized; make it the best offering of your creative vision, talents and skills.

CREATIVE BINDER
PERSONAL
STATEMENT

Many schools request a letter of intent, also known as a personal statement. A well-crafted personal statement can greatly influence the decision of a panel. This is a golden opportunity to introduce yourself in writing and make them want to meet you.

The emphasis here is on *personal*. This essay is about you—and only you can write it. Craft an engaging summary of who you are, where you're from, what you've done and why you are the perfect candidate for their program.

Write about your skills and what you've done to develop them;

List your interests and describe how you've pursued them;

Expand on your abilities and how they are relevant to your goals as a filmmaker.

This is a chance to send a clear message of your talents. You want to sell your strengths, convey your goals and underline your passions. Be specific. Don't dilute your statement with unnecessary information.

BONUS TIP:

If you can write about how you came to your decision to apply to their film school by weaving in a story, an anecdote, or an insightful experience that shows your individuality and imagination, do it!

. . . .

CREATIVE WORK

The scope of creative expression in art, film and media is far-reaching. Portfolios can include a variety of materials: paintings, sculptures, installations, set design, costume design, or anything that you've created.

Aside from films, screenplays and writing samples, most other forms of creative work will likely be submitted as photographs. Whether it's a costume you've designed or a model you've sculpted, the photos should be the best possible presentation of your work.

Imagine being on a portfolio assessment panel and reviewing hundreds or thousands of photographs. Like everyone, you know the good ones when you see them. You're drawn to them; they make you feel something. Strong images make people want to look closer.

There are different techniques and approaches for composing frames that grab and hold someone's attention. Research and study images that you find striking, memorable and evocative. Note the details, content and design elements that shape your emotional reaction: colour, line, rhythm, shape, space and tone.

Lighting is key. For production designers, a good set looks much better when it's lit. Sure, you can grab a picture with your smartphone—but lighting can make the photograph. Shadows, highlights and reflections all contribute to the feel and power of an image.

How you present your work speaks to your standards of professionalism and attention to detail. For the school, it's a first look at the kind of student that you intend to be.

If the work you are presenting *is* your photography, it has to be exceptional.

DEMO REEL

If you plan to submit a film or demo reel in your portfolio, make it as good as it can be. A well-crafted short—under five minutes—could be the deciding factor that makes you stand out from the crowd.

Making a film shows that you really want to be there. It sends a strong message about your ambition, your potential, and the likelihood for you to succeed in a production program. Committees respect the effort that goes into making a film, particularly when there are limited resources. If it's a good story, it doesn't matter if you've shot it on a smartphone.

In any given year, top schools receive hundreds of films. Yours will be compared to others. You might apply with an exceptionally strong portfolio only to find yourself in a particularly competitive year where the school has more talented candidates than they have room for. This happens with film festivals, too.

If you've made a film, great! If you've made a few films then you'll have to decide on which one you like best or how you might cut together a montage: an assembly of short, dramatic scenes with good performances. If you're aiming for a particular specialization like cinematography, you may want to select scenes with your best lighting, camera moves and compositions.

If you haven't made a film, I don't recommend that you rush out and shoot something in order to satisfy a submission requirement. A rushed film will come off as feeling just that—rushed. Making a good film depends on many factors. If it's your first film, think more about 'what' you want to shoot and 'how' you want to shoot it before you shoot anything.

Your film should reflect your interests, tastes and abilities. Whether you are applying to a narrative, experimental or documentary program—your film should demonstrate your talents and filmmaking sensibilities. Be careful with 'talking head' interviews as they are not always strong indicators of visual storytelling. Even the most compelling story told by an interview subject does not help a selection committee evaluate you as a filmmaker.

WRITING SAMPLE

Programs that focus on narrative filmmaking may ask for a creative writing sample, usually a short script. This is an opportunity to showcase your ability to tell a simple visual story in a clear, direct fashion.

Here are some screenplay assessment categories to consider:

> **Format** – is the script in proper master scene format?
>
> **Clarity** – is the story clear?
>
> **Genre** – does the story fall into a defined genre?
>
> **Originality** – has it been done before?

Structure – is there a beginning, middle, and end? Is there a twist?

Momentum – is it a good, well-paced read?

Characters – are they unique, engaging, and relatable?

Dialogue – do characters have distinct voices?

Forces of antagonism – are the obstacles and challenges substantial?

You may have heard that people in the industry won't even read your whole script. Expect the same response with portfolio submissions. You may have a good story, but there is a craft to writing a screenplay. For the informed reader, your command of the screenwriting craft is evident in the first few pages.

To write better scripts, read more scripts.

BRAND

Films schools are looking for outstanding, creative individuals. The application process is your opportunity to give people a clear sense of who you are: your talent, determination and vision. When the competition gets tough, a strong, consistent message of your unique brand can make the difference.

Building your brand starts with understanding how other people see you. Your brand is your character, your style and what you're known for. Along with your application materials, the message you send with your appearance, behaviour and body language speaks volumes.

Film school can be a place to develop your professional reputation, but first things first: you have to get in. Top-ranked university programs require you to jump through a lot of hoops before you walk the hallowed halls. One of the first things you need to provide is your academic transcript: a copy of your permanent academic record of all courses taken, all grades received and your educational accomplishments, such as honours and degrees.

Universities usually have a GPA requirement. If you cross this threshold, great! The subsequent steps allow you absolute control over the content you present—and how you present yourself. If you haven't got the grades, there's nothing you can do to change the evidence on your record.

Some programs put a greater emphasis on portfolios, life experience and interviews. Having a sense of self and an awareness of your place in the world is a strong foundation for storytelling. Admission committees want to know about the raw materials you'll source as a storyteller. The stories you want to tell are more important than the movies you like to watch.

If you haven't put much thought into the idea of your brand, this is something you can start building at any point in time. Every class, every interaction and every email is an opportunity to make a memorable impression. Being affable, honest and trustworthy is the starting point for building good relationships. Having a sense of humour will always serve you well, too.

People notice when you try hard and put your top efforts into everything you do. That's how the best brands are built. That's what you want to be known for.

WRITTEN COMMUNICATIONS

We're in a fast-paced world: deadlines are tight and prompt responses are required. You need to be an effective communicator or you'll struggle to advance in any professional capacity.

Emails are a convenient and powerful tool, and they need to be used wisely. Always remember that emails can be forwarded to anyone without your knowledge or approval. They can also be kept on file forever. Like any written document, craft your message with carefully chosen words. The language you use and how you present your position creates a chemical reaction in the brain of the reader. Think about how you might react to an email that was full of typos and bad grammar.

Written communications will likely precede a personal meeting. How you write a request for an interview, or how you respond, can set the tone for that meeting.

THE 6 C'S OF EMAIL COMPOSITION

Good emails stand out. They are noticed and appreciated. At a professional level, they are mandatory. If you apply these easy-to-remember 6C's, you'll be off to a good start:

1. **CORRECT** – Typos can hurt your credibility: incorrect spelling, poor grammar and faulty punctuation are avoidable. Get someone to check important messages;

2. **CLEAR** – Ambiguity, confusion and uncertainty are not the objectives for an effective communicator;

3. **CONCISE** – Use fewer words. Get to the point. Be accurate and precise. You can expand on your thoughts later;

4. **COMPLETE** – Provide all of the details, questions and info in one email, rather than sending a series of emails with 'Oh, one more thing…';

5. **CORDIAL** – It is always possible to be polite, thoughtful and kind. This isn't about sugarcoating a message, it's about being professional;

6. **CLOSING** – Make sure you sign off in a manner that is appropriate for the relationship and content. Emails that close with 'Thanks,' 'Thanks in advance,' or 'Thank you' generate more responses—and better brain chemistry for the reader.

PERSONAL MEETINGS

Human interaction—live and in-person—is under siege. Technology has sidelined the art of conversation. Take a stroll across any campus and you'll find more students engaged with their smartphones than with people sitting right next to them.

The age of emails and texting has resulted in fewer face-to-face meetings, which doesn't help you develop better interpersonal skills. It's hard to improve if you don't have the opportunities to practice. Developing your meeting skills and presenting a position is imperative for becoming a strong contributor in a key creative role on a film production. You need to be able to present well in every situation.

Meetings require strategy. First off, you have to know whose meeting it is. It also helps to know the agenda items and time allotted for those items in order to be appropriately prepared.

You need to know who's in the room and what's at stake. Understanding the hierarchy of those in attendance helps you frame your approach. It can shape your ideas on what needs to be communicated and how to organize your participation. Remember, first impressions count!

For every important meeting, there are four fundamental factors to keep in mind:

what you hear;
what you say;
how you say it;
and what you don't say.

Interviews are an important stage in the selection process when the number of applicants is greater than the number of available seats. If you get the call for an interview—congratulations! This means that you've made the short list and meeting you is the last piece of the puzzle for making their decisions. You should be thoroughly prepared.

Well ahead of the scheduled meeting, do as much relevant research on the school as you possibly can: the faculty, the administration, the alumni, etc. Gather any materials that you may want to leave behind at the conclusion of the interview. Having extra copies of your resume or other key written documents is always a good idea.

A personal interview is your best opportunity to make a good impression. Your appearance, attitude and level of preparedness will be closely observed.

The committee is looking for well-rounded, creative individuals who can thrive in a team-learning environment. You should be eager to discuss all aspects of your submission: your portfolio, creative interests and long-term goals. Be ready for anything: you may be asked to pitch an original idea for a film that you would like to make in the program.

Clarity, insight and demeanour are standard criteria upon which applicants are judged. Pre-think the situation carefully. What are your best answers for the most likely questions? What might some of the tough questions be?

I've sat on committees with colleagues who feel that every applicant must be challenged. They push; they raise the stakes; they want to see you think on the spot. They ask 'trick' questions, "If you were a boat, what kind of boat would you be?" I'm not fan of this approach but I've seen it happen. If it happens to you, have some fun with it. Be original. Be imaginative. It's not about having the right answers; it's about the willingness to work towards the answers. Don't dismiss an interview question.

Committees may offer the applicant the chance to ask them questions. This is an indirect opportunity for you to let them know that you've done your homework on the program. If you do ask a question, be genuinely interested in the answer. Show that you are a good communicator by being a good listener.

I've been in some important interviews that went sideways—fast. How can you improve your chances for keeping things on a positive roll? Well, it never hurts to practice. Family and friends are the usual suspects to ask for help with this. Ask them to really grill you. It's better to stumble now.

Since you're going to film school, why not take this rehearsal process one step further and film yourself answering questions. Watching yourself is a great way to learn and practice. It helps you chart your improvement and gauge your readiness. You can review it alone or watch it with friends and family. Getting input and criticism will help you be stronger in the interview.

Search the internet to find interview tutorials, sample questions and coaching ideas. This is what other candidates are doing. Once you've decided on a list of questions, write your answers down. Edit them. Revise them. Get second opinions.

You could also try doing a bit of mirror work as you practice different versions of your answers. Sit in front of a mirror and watch yourself as you rehearse. This can help with confidence and relaxation.

If you get the chance to peek inside an animation studio you'll see that every character animator has a mirror on their desk to try out different facial expressions. Actors, athletes and dancers all do mirror work to study, practice and improve. At the very least, they may realize what they might be doing wrong.

PROFESSIONALISM

There is only one person who is responsible for your professionalism. Actions, words and choices are all decisions that you make of your own volition. Work ethic and attitude are important qualities that impact your chances for success. Showing up late or unprepared does not go over well on any job.

Schools have varying expectations for attendance and engagement, but you won't find much flexibility in the industry: people get fired for not conducting themselves professionally. Schools set their own standards and grading criteria. In some courses, professionalism (sometimes referred to as participation) can be up to 20 percent of the final mark.

Standard criteria for professionalism is laid out in four categories:

Attendance

Engagement

Participation

Deliverables

Professionalism is vital for your personal brand and long-term success in any career. Film is no different. In order to achieve your goals, you may have to address bad habits and take steps to correct them. Compulsive phone use, chronic tardiness, and unreliability are things that you have control over, but this isn't what you should be going to film school to learn.

Some schools don't give professionalism the emphasis that it deserves. Professional behaviour will be essential for career advancement in life after film school. Consistency is something to strive for. It can take years to build a good reputation—and seconds to lose it. As the saying goes: good news travels slowly, bad news travels fast.

A good film education embraces the industry expectations for respectful treatment of everyone involved in the making of a film. A program that provides real-world production scenarios can help smooth out the transition from student to working professional.

TOO COOL FOR SCHOOL

I had a student who arrived 30 minutes late for the first class of a new term. Finding the right room can be confusing on day one.

Next class, same thing. Everyone was seated and we were well into the lecture. He showed up late with a coffee, checked his phone, looked out the window and whispered to the student next to him about what he'd missed. After finishing his coffee, he got tired and closed his eyes.

He strolled in even later for the third class.

"We started 45 minutes ago," I said. "I'd appreciate you being on time."

"I'm paying to be here," he replied. "I'll be on time when I'm getting paid to be on time."

His classmates exchanged silent looks, not a smile in the group.

Jeopardizing your relationships with colleagues and teachers creates unnecessary complications.

Filmmaking is teamwork. Understanding what it means to be a team player, even if you're a star, is vital for good working relationships and the overall success of the team's performance. Good teams make good films.

Long story short, he didn't complete the program.

PART V

FINAL NOTES

Film school is like an obstacle course:

it's challenging and difficult, and

if you had the chance to do it a second time,

you'd probably do remarkably better.

*I think one of the privileges of being
a filmmaker is the opportunity to
remain a kind of perpetual student.*

— EDWARD ZWICK

*Having a real understanding of history,
literature, science and psychology is very
important to being able to make movies.*

— GEORGE LUCAS

*The most valuable of all education
is the ability to make yourself do the
thing you have to do, when it has to
be done, whether you like it or not.*

— ALDOUS HUXLEY

DO IT RIGHT THE FIRST TIME

The approach for PRIMER is straightforward: to provide you with insight, information and strategies, in advance of going to film school, in order to help you plan a positive educational experience and make good films. The more information you have, the more prepared you'll be for making decisions that are right for you. The objective of this book is to help you generate creative assets, shape your learning goals, and develop your soft skills.

Film school is like an obstacle course: it's challenging and difficult, and if you had the chance to do it a second time, you'd probably do remarkably better. Working through PRIMER is like walking through the obstacles of a film program at your own pace. Once you know what to expect, you are better prepared to hit the ground running on your way to realizing your best film education experience.

Film schools provide the training and opportunity for you to write, direct and shoot your own films. Student filmmaking mirrors the situations you'll encounter in the professional independent industry. Managing your resources, scheduling all phases of the production and finishing a film to a deadline is about as real as it gets.

You'll learn many things in film school, but you'll want to leave with an understanding of the filmmaker's mindset: the balance of knowledge, experience and confidence that you need to draw on when you make a film. Your time in film school is uniquely yours. Filmmaking is risk-taking—but film education doesn't have to be. It's as simple as this:

Be as prepared as possible.

You set the standard for what you want to accomplish during your film school adventure. If you have a goal and you believe you can accomplish it, then there is only the work ahead to do. Aim to complete it to the best of your abilities.

Filmmaking is a journey. You want to make the right choices at the right time for you; choices that you're happy with; choices that will help you thrive in your film career. Going to film school with goals, ideas and stories that you are passionate about, and then seeing those ideas and stories transform into films is how you showcase your talents and stand out from the crowd.

This book is about taking charge of your destiny by taking advantage of your education—rather than your education taking advantage of you. Meeting the academic challenges and maximizing your creativity while fighting off doubt, debt and fatigue is hard—if not daunting—for anyone. You have to be forward thinking; you have to visualize; you have to anticipate. If you've given each exercise here your complete attention, you'll avoid the pitfalls and dodge the common mistakes that derail the most enthusiastic and eager students.

After 100 years, the guiding principles for the training and development of the filmmakers of tomorrow still hold true. Promoting innovation, creativity and voice in a supportive community are, and always will be, the cornerstones of film education. Connecting with other filmmakers while pursuing your own personalized curriculum is what elevates the 21st century film student experience.

Be yourself—reflect your inner truths.

Nurture your thoughts and ideas—help them grow and flourish.

Enjoy what you create—otherwise your efforts will be pointless.

Embrace your imagination—this is your Source. Protect it.

DON'T LET GRADES DEFINE YOU

Learning to work with actors is a fundamental aspect of a film director's education. For my term project in my final directing course as a student, I chose to do a scene from an original feature screenplay. The script was something I was planning to produce and direct in the coming year, so this was a no-nonsense exercise.

The student actors were wonderful, and I was a one-man DIY crew: staging, lighting, directing, shooting and editing. It was a fun and enjoyable learning experience. When it came time to screen it, I got a positive reception from everyone except the teacher: he gave me the lowest mark in the class.

Despite the poor grade, I went on to realize my dream of producing and directing that script. It served as my MFA thesis project, but it also became the first feature-length film completed in a graduate program in Canada. *The Grocer's Wife* premiered at the Toronto International Film Festival and received a special jury citation for best Canadian film.

Months later, the phone rang with more wonderful news: the film had been selected to open the Critic's Week at the Cannes International Film Festival, the most prestigious showcase in the world. It received a great review in *Variety*, was honoured with international awards, and went on to win two Canadian academy awards for best supporting actress (Nicola Cavendish) and best first feature.

Meanwhile, back at school, I received a diploma and graduated. Upon reviewing my transcript, I couldn't help but notice that my teacher was still not impressed. He gave my film a 'B'.

The important lesson that I pass on to all my students is that in order to grow as a filmmaker and creative spirit, you have to learn to trust your instincts: trust that little voice inside. Everything you create and bring to the attention of others will be met with both positive and negative reactions. It is all part of the journey.

When you harness the energy of your passions and proceed with determination and conviction, anything is possible. Trust and commit.

And don't let grades define you.

CREATIVE BINDER CHECKLIST

MISSION STATEMENT

TALENTS & INTERESTS

     List of Interests

     List of Talents

     List of Skills

     List of Film-Related Skills

     List of Creative Talents for Portfolio Assets

SMART GOALS

     List of Career Goals

     Strategy to Achieve Career Goals

     Education Goals

     Timeline

FILM SCHOOL CRITERIA

     Evaluation Priority

     Evaluation Chart

SCHOOL SELECTION

     Information and Research on Top Picks

FINANCING & COSTS

     School Scholarships, Bursaries, and Grants

     Alternative Sources for Financing

     School Financing Support for Films

     School Equipment Support

     Project Cost Estimates

     Budget & Financing Flowchart

PART V FINAL NOTES

ADVANCE HOMEWORK SCHEDULE

    Film Screening and Research Schedule

'MUST READ' BOOK LIST

FROM SCRIPT TO SCREEN

    Notes on Scripts and Films

'TOP FILMS' LIST

    List of Top 10, 25 or 50 Films

FILM STUDIES

    Notes on Films, Select Scenes, and Research

PECHA KUCHA

    Concepts for Presentations

    Completed Presentation

PHOTOGRAPHY – 24 FRAMES

STORYBOARDS

    List of Shots

    Hand Drawn Frames to Match Shots

    Arrows to Suggest Movement

STORY IDEA GENERATOR

    Notes and Short Descriptions

SCENE OUTLINES

    Detailed Notes and Descriptions

30 MINUTE DRILL

    Exercises for Story Development

SHORT SCRIPTS

Five to Seven Page Formatted Scripts

PERSONAL STATEMENT

Letter of Intent for Pursuing Film Education

SELECT LINKS

There are excellent online forums and websites for film education and ongoing professional development. Here are a few of my favourites:

Every Frame a Painting – a series of video essays about film form, made from April 2014 to September 2016, by Taylor Ramos and Tony Zhou.

www.youtube.com/everyframeapainting

The Nerdwriter – a weekly video essay series on film, art, culture and more, created by writer/director/producer Evan Puschak.

www.youtube.com/Nerdwriter1

Crash Course – an educational YouTube channel with short videos on film history, criticism, and production.

www.youtube.com/crashcourse

No Film School – a hub that posts the latest tutorials, interviews, short films, and gear news to help filmmakers learn from each other.

https://nofilmschool.com/

https://www.youtube.com/user/nofilmschool

Screen Prism – entertaining, insightful video essays and articles on films and television.

screenprism.com/

www.youtube.com/screenprism

Cinephilia & Beyond – a website dedicated to the world of film.

cinephiliabeyond.org/

Film School Rejects – A blog devoted to movie reviews, interviews, film industry news, and feature commentary. It was founded by Neil Miller in February 2006.

filmschoolrejects.com/

Action Cut Print – The banner reads: filmmaking tips for the independent filmmaker. A film directing resource center, website hub, and free monthly e-zine read by filmmakers in over 100 countries. Founded by Peter Marshall.

actioncutprint.com/

Drew's Script-O-Rama - A great site for free scripts and screenplays, founded in 1995. There are screenplays available on other sites, but this is where I usually go first.

www.script-o-rama.com

APPENDICES

SELECT BIBLIOGRAPHY

Block, Alex B., Wilson, Lucy A. *George Lucas's Blockbusting: A Decade-by-Decade Survey of Timeless Movies including Untold Secrets of their Financial and Cultural Success* (New York: HarperCollins Publishers, 2010)

Covey, Stephen R. *The 7 Habits of Highly Effective People: Powerful Lessons in Personal Change* (Free Press/Simon & Schuster, 1989)

Goldman, William. *Adventures in the Screen Trade: A Personal View of Hollywood and Screenwriting*, 15th edition. (New York: Grand Central Publishing, 1989)

Henri, Robert. *The Art Spirit* (New York: Harper & Row, 1984)

Lynch, David. *Catching the Big Fish: Meditation, Consciousness, and Creativity* (New York: Penguin Group, 2007)

Mascelli, Joseph V. *The Five C's of Cinematography: Motion Picture Filming Techniques Simplified* (Los Angeles: Silman-James Press, 2005)

Murch, Walter. *In the Blink of an Eye: A Perspective on Film Editing* (Los Angeles: Silman-James Press, 2007)

Ondaatje, Michael. *The Conversations: Walter Murch and the Art of Editing Film* (New York: Alfred A. Knopf Publisher, 2002)

Palmer, Parker J. *The Courage to Teach: Exploring the Inner Landscape of a Teacher's Life* (San Francisco: John Wiley & Sons, 1998)

Proferes, Nicholas T. *Film Directing Fundamentals: See Your Film Before Shooting* (New York, London: Focal Press, Taylor & Francis Group, 2008)

Spaner, David. *Dreaming in the Rain: How Vancouver Became Hollywood North by Northwest.* (Arsenal Pulp Press, 2003)

Truffaut, Francois. *Hitchcock Truffaut.* (New York: Simon & Schuster, 1967)

GLOSSARY OF ACADEMIC TERMS

Accreditation

Official certification that a school or course has met standards set by external regulators. Accrediting bodies are managed by various organizations and have different standards.

Adjunct Professor

A part-time teacher employed in higher education for a specific purpose, particular class, or length of time.

Curriculum

The lessons and subjects comprising a course of study or program in a school.

GPA

Abbreviation for grade point average. A number representing the average value of the accumulated grades earned in academic courses.

Net Price Calculator

An online tool for financial aid calculation to help prospective students estimate the total contribution required for one or more years at a post-secondary institution. Every college in the U.S. that offers federal student aid is required to have their own web-based version. Remember, it's only an estimate! (See Student Loan Calculator.)

Portfolio

A gathering or selection of creative work provided to accompany applications.

Scholarship

A grant, award, or payment made to support a student's education, based on academic or other achievement.

Student Loan Calculator

A financial aid tool to estimate the monthly payments for a loan over time, including the principal and total interest paid.

Syllabus

An outline of the lessons, learning materials, subjects, and grading in a course of study, usually distributed on the first day of class.

University

A high-level educational institution where students study for degrees across many different faculties and professional schools.

Vocational School

An educational institution designed to provide technical training and skills required to perform the tasks of a particular job, specialization, or trade.

Workshop

An educational program or class for a relatively small group that focuses on techniques and skills in a particular field or specialization.

GLOSSARY OF SCREENWRITING TERMS

Action

The scene description, character movement, and sounds as described in a screenplay. Written below the scene heading or 'slugline'.

Backstory

The history, real or fictional, of a character in a story. It may be suggested or implied, but not necessarily included, in the written text. Actors may invent a backstory for their character.

Character

A role in a story, play, or film. In a screenplay that adheres to master scene format, the name appears in all caps the first time a character is introduced in the "Action." The character's name can then be written normally in the rest of the script.

Dialogue

The words that characters are supposed to say according to the script. In master scene format, dialogue is written in a narrow center margin and clearly labeled by the character who is speaking the words.

Dramatic tension

An excitement and anticipation created and maintained primarily through conflict. An important element to all forms of fiction and film.

EXT.

An abbreviation for Exterior, used for screenplay formatting. This scene takes place outdoors. Listed in the scene heading or 'slugline', this information facilitates scheduling and budgeting.

Fast Writing

A timed exercise of writing in a freewheeling approach to generate as much information as you can, as fast as you can, about the highlights, main points, details, or story ideas for a project.

Genre

A category of film, such as comedy or horror, characterized by similarities in tone, visual style, narrative techniques, and subject matter.

INT.

An abbreviation for Interior, used for screenplay formatting. This scene takes place indoors. See EXT.

Master Scene Format

The industry standard for writing screenplays. A formatting style that breaks the story into scenes, not cuts. Very simply, there is a scene heading (also known as a slugline), a descriptive paragraph of the action, and dialogue, if necessary.

Narrative Structure

In the most basic definition, a three-act structure has the beginning, middle and end of a story, or the set-up, development, and resolution.

POV

Abbreviation for Point of View. When the camera replaces the eyes of a character, surveillance camera, or other device to see the world through that unique, privileged perspective.

Scene

A dramatic situation with a beginning, middle, and end, that takes place at the same time and in the same location.

Script

A general term for the written manuscript that precedes the making of a film, and is used by the creative team to visualize the story, characters, setting, and dialogue. Also known as a screenplay.

Sequence

A major phase of action in a screenplay, such as the wedding sequence in *The Godfather*.

Slugline

A header appearing in a script before each scene or shot detailing the location and time that the action is intended to occur in. The text is in all CAPS. Also known as a Scene Heading.

Storytelling

The act of sharing a narrative, a tale, or a series of events in an entertaining and effective manner. A social and cultural activity to engage, educate, and present moral values and beliefs to a community.

Subtext

What is thought, the inner world of the character. The thoughts, beliefs, and ideas underneath the spoken dialogue.

Synopsis

A short summary or condensed statement of a story or film that gives a brief outline of the plot, characters, and subject matter.

Text

The written words of a script, including the dialogue of the characters, descriptions of the action, and information about their outer world.

GLOSSARY OF FILMMAKING TERMS

Bird's Eye Diagram

Overhead perspective drawings used for illustrating a floor plan or layout.

Blocking

The working out of the movement and details of the actor and camera, as determined by what's important in the scene.

Boom Microphone

A telescoping pole with a microphone on the end to extend near the actors while keeping the boom operator out of frame.

Choreography

A sequence of planned steps and arranged movements in a dance or creative routine.

Composition

The placement or arrangement of visual elements in a picture or photograph.

Craft Service

The coffee, drinks, snacks, fruit, etc. that a crew can grab on set while they are working.

Crowdfunding

The funding of a project by raising small amounts of money from a large number of people, typically via the internet.

Demo Reel

Demo is short for 'demonstration' – a visual compilation of filmmaking expertise to show a sample of work by directors, cinematographers, visual effects artists, designers, etc.

Director

The person who visualizes the movie based on the script, creates shots, suggests how the actors should portray their characters, and helps to edit the final cut.

Feature Film

The main attraction for a cinema or theatre, a long-form filmed story over one hour in length that patrons pay to see.

Film Ratings

A system used by a country or territory to rate a film's suitability for certain audiences based on its content, including specific age restrictions and warnings for violence, sexual imagery, or profane language.

Fix it in Post

The term used when something doesn't go as planned during principle photography but no effort is made to re-shoot or correct it, suggesting or hoping that the shot can be repaired or re-done in post-production.

Foley

The recording of custom sound effects during post-production, such as footsteps, doors opening, etc.

Improvisation

An unexpected or impromptu performance, composition, or execution of anything without previous preparation.

Landscape Orientation

A photography, word-processing, and publishing term that refers to the document or photo being wider than it is tall, oriented horizontally.

Lighting Plan

The type and position of lights on a set or location, determined by the cinematographer.

Location Permit

The authorization from the owner of a property to allow filming.

Period Film

A film story set in a different time or era, not a contemporary setting.

Pitch

A personal presentation of an idea that you are seeking approval for or trying to persuade others to support.

Post-Production

The final stage of the filmmaking process. Work performed on a movie after the end of principle photography, usually editing, sound, and visual effects.

Pre-Production

The preparation or planning period, completing the activities and details that are necessary in order to shoot the film.

Principle Photography

The filming of major or significant components of a movie which involve lead actors.

Production

The phase of filmmaking during which principle photography occurs.

Prop

Anything that an actor touches or uses on the set: pen, briefcase, cutlery, cup, etc.

Rack Focus

A change of focus within the frame, to shift attention, to show the audience what to look at.

Schematics

Overhead, bird's eye diagrams to depict the layout of the character positions, camera placements, or their movement for a shot or a scene.

Score

The musical component of a film soundtrack

Shot

From the first to last frame that the camera shoots. The images gathered from when the director says "action" to "cut."

Shot List

Very simply, a list of all the camera angles, shot sizes, and shots needed for a shoot.

Storyboard

A series of drawings or images displayed in chronological order, used to help film directors visualize a scene, especially for scenes with stunts, action, or visual effects components.

Take

Multiple versions of the same shot are called takes.

Vision Statement

A description of how the director intends to realize the script in a cinematic form: the style of the film, the tone, the visual look, the production design, the editing, the sound design, the music, etc.

Wrap or "It's a Wrap!"

The term for when you have completed shooting for the day, for the set, or on the entire film.

ACKNOWLEDGEMENTS

Writing this book has been a journey of discovery and collaboration. I am deeply grateful for all of the guidance, help and support that I've received along the way. The process has been similar to making an independent feature film: countless hours at the keyboard, months of planning and research, and doing whatever it takes to reach a common goal with a team of talented people. I am truly fortunate to have had such a satisfying and wonderful experience.

My heartfelt thanks and love to Lorraine Jamison, my partner-in-everything. Love and thanks to my brother, Jim, and all of my family for their support and feedback. To my eagle-eyed editors, Justin Gagnon and Matthew Gagnon: working with you has been a rewarding experience. Thank you for your expertise, your attention to detail, and for making the work better. And an additional shout out to Matthew for designing the book cover and chapter graphics.

I want to acknowledge and thank my colleagues and former students who inspired me to reflect on the content of various drafts. To Hans Christian Berger, David Roncin, Jake Warren, Sebastien de Castell, Oscar Pietri, Robert

French, Scott Watson, Will Meadows, Tyler Deck, Tony Zhou, Matt Shaw, Jessica Cole, Chris Cowden, Jake Hiltz, Olga Madelave, Nick Meunier, Ramiya Pusharajah, Micah Sharkey, David Spaven, Tane Stang, and Connor Tkachuk: your notes and encouragement were invaluable.

A resounding thank you to all who were willing to jump into early drafts and agree to be on the advanced reader team: Adam Wood, Amir Houshang Hashemi, Andrea Gonzalez Carrillo, Arlein Perez Garcia, Arlene Arnold, Ben Calaf, Brandon Arkesteyn, Brian Kaufmann, Cameron Tremblay, Chris Fuller, Christie Will Wolf, Colin Kozachuk, Connor Smith, Craig McEwen, Daniel Baker, David Vardanyan, Dubin Kim, Dwayne Beaver, Eric Dermanouelian, Fernanda Figueroa, Greg Coyes, Hayden Woodhead, Himmat Sarkaria, Jaselle Martino, Jaz Shaw, Javier Arenales, Joel Kennedy, Kathian Pascal, Kevin Shah, Kevin Tseng, Lesley Cazares, Marc Aubin, Mark Anthony Hogan, Mark Lemmon, Matthew Richards, Mitchell Kezin, Mohamad El Masri, Nate Draper, Pat McEleney, Peter Marshall, Rasha Amer, Ritchie Lyon, Roger Fires, Rosalee Yagihara, Roxana Pief, Ryan Bonder, Salman Sajun, Sean Meek, Shaun Rykiss, Tara Dafoe, Victoria Pearson, Vignesh Rajagolpalan, Walter Gasparovic, and Zakim Nuraney.

Thank you to the team at Tellwell for your publishing assistance.

And to my students: my utmost appreciation for the opportunity to learn from each and every one of you. Our time together continues to be a treasure trove of insight, experience and newfound knowledge. Thank you!

MEET THE AUTHOR

Photo by Jake Warren

John Pozer is an award-winning independent filmmaker whose features have premiered at top international festivals, such as Cannes, Sundance and Toronto. In his 30-plus years of industry experience, he has directed stories ranging from crime mysteries to teen comedies to supernatural dramas for major networks, including The Disney Channel, MTV, and Fox Family. He earned a Master of Fine Arts degree from Concordia University in Montreal, and has taught over 1,000 students as a senior instructor at Vancouver Film School and adjunct professor at Simon Fraser University, The Art Institutes, LaSalle College, British Columbia Institute of Technology, and the University of British Columbia. Visit him at www.pozervision.com.